The Conscious Caregiver

A Mindful Approach to Caring for Your Loved One *Without Losing Yourself*

The Conscious Caregiver

A Mindful Approach to Caring for Your Loved One *Without Losing Yourself*

LINDA ABBIT

Adams Media
New York London Toronto Sydney New Delhi

Adams Media
An Imprint of Simon & Schuster, Inc.
57 Littlefield Street
Avon, Massachusetts 02322

First Adams Media trade paperback edition SEPTEMBER 2017

Interior design by Heather McKiel

Manufactured in the United States of America

10 9 8 7 6 5 4

Library of Congress Cataloging-in-Publication Data
Abbit, Linda, author.
The conscious caregiver / Linda Abbit.
Avon, Massachusetts: Adams Media, 2017.
Includes index.
LCCN 2017021313 (print) | LCCN 2017026689 (ebook) | ISBN 9781440597732 (pb) | ISBN 9781440597749 (ebook)
LCSH: Caregivers. | Caregivers--Mental health. | Home care services. | BISAC: FAMILY & RELATIONSHIPS / Eldercare. | FAMILY & RELATIONSHIPS / Aging. | SELF-HELP / Aging.
LCC RA973.5 (ebook) | LCC RA973.5 .A23 2017 (print) | DDC 362.14--dc23
LC record available at https://lccn.loc.gov/2017021313

ISBN 978-1-4405-9773-2
ISBN 978-1-4405-9774-9 (ebook)

DEDICATION

For my parents, Aida and Al Brodsky, who modeled what caregiving is and allowed me the honor of caring for them.

For Robbie, who adds a wonderful dimension to my world and is the light of my life.

For Jeff, who supports me every step of the way—in everything I undertake—and provides much love and laughter daily. I could never have done this without you!

TABLE OF CONTENTS

PART 2

PART 3

ACKNOWLEDGMENTS

Thank you to the family caregivers interviewed for this book for so generously sharing your time and intimate family stories with me. I also appreciate the many other caregivers, both family and professional, I've met over the years. You are all my heroes.

I especially want to thank Steve and Marsha Bisheff, Barbara Aria, Helene Moore, Vicki Olivadoti, Barbara Swafford, Ed Dale, Michelle Seitzer, Ernie and Nadine Abbit, Faye Abbit, and Aileen Sherman (of blessed memory) for your unwavering belief in me and your help in making this book a reality.

INTRODUCTION

"There are only four kinds of people in the world: those who have been caregivers, those who are currently caregivers, those who will be caregivers, and those who will need caregivers."

—Rosalynn Carter, First Lady of the US and president of the Rosalynn Carter Institute for Caregiving

Caregiving for a loved one is made up of special times filled with love, devotion, and compassion. And caregiving can bring opportunities to learn more about your own character and your loved one. But caregiving is also filled with huge responsibilities, exhausting days, struggles, and worries—and caregivers often find themselves wrestling with burnout, guilt, and high levels of stress.

It should come as no surprise that a physically and emotionally healthy caregiver is automatically a better caregiver, but how can you take care of yourself when you're so busy taking care of someone else? Enter *The Conscious Caregiver.*

Here you'll learn to use mindfulness techniques to pause, notice exactly what is happening around you, and then respond in a way that is a win-win for both you and your loved one. You'll also find a variety of ways to practice self-care every day, even if you have only five minutes to accomplish it. By using these techniques and others like them, you'll learn how to become a more relaxed, focused, confident, and, most importantly, conscious caregiver. Your care recipient and your family will not be the only ones who will notice and appreciate your positive attitude and calm approach—you'll benefit greatly too!

How do I know so much about conscious caregiving? In addition to working in the eldercare field and volunteering for the Alzheimer's Association, I was a caregiver to both of my parents. As their caregiver for more than ten years, I faced many of the questions that you've either experienced or may experience in the future, including:

- How can I practice self-care?
- How do I know if I should move my loved one from his or her home, and when is the right time?
- How do I deal with the guilt and sadness I feel?
- How can I use mindful communication to talk with my loved one about sensitive topics?
- What is hospice, and what does this service provide?
- What do I do after caregiving ends?

Throughout this book you'll find answers to these questions and more. You'll also find a variety of case studies that show how other people have and are dealing with their caregiving struggles. Finally, I'll provide a number of exercises that will help you step back, be mindful, and figure out the best way to take care of your loved one.

The highs and lows along your caregiving journey will be unique to your particular care recipient's and family's situation. But whether you're currently caregiving or are soon to be, whether you're taking care of a loved one from far away or from your very own home, whether you're taking care of your parents and your own kids at the same time, this book will show you how to embrace the importance of self-care and how to make time to be the most conscious caregiver you can be. Good luck on your journey.

PART 1

What Is Conscious Caregiving?

CHAPTER 1

Your Role As a Conscious Caregiver

Family caregivers have multiple jobs. In a single day, you can go from being a chef and chauffeur to a nurse and medical advocate, and every day can be different. In this chapter, you will learn why it's important to self-identify sooner rather than later as your loved one's caregiver, how caregiving affects your emotional state, and how your care recipient's emotional status changes as she ages. You'll also examine the impact of role reversal and role confusion as a result of these new family dynamics.

But first we'll take a look at what it really means to be a conscious caregiver and how that identifier influences everything else you do when taking care of your loved one. Conscious caregivers direct time, energy, and compassion toward themselves as well as their care recipients. Here you'll learn how to apply mindfulness techniques to become more aware of your state of being during caregiving situations.

WHAT IS CONSCIOUS CAREGIVING?

Becoming a caregiver can happen overnight due to a sudden health change, or it might creep up on you slowly. Your loved one may be experiencing the physical decline that comes with normal aging, may be having memory loss issues, or both. But while these situations are difficult, if you're fortunate, one day you will find yourself in the role of family caregiver.

Family caregivers wear many hats. You might be a chauffeur, nurse, companion, physical therapist, cook, housekeeper, banker, financial planner, medical liaison, personal assistant (bathing, grooming, toileting), and social director. You might also become "roommates" for all or part of your caregiving journey together.

At first, you may be helping with grocery shopping weekly, checking in with your loved one by phone or a visit after your workday, or reviewing his or her financial statements monthly. Then your assistance may increase either due to his requests or because you recognize new needs your loved one has. The earlier you identify that you've started on your caregiving journey, the sooner you can think about and plan for the future. This might involve lining up local resources, becoming educated about aging overall or your loved one's specific health problem, and/or joining a support group. Whatever responsibilities you face now and in the future, approaching them as a conscious caregiver will allow your journey to go more smoothly.

So what is a conscious caregiver? Conscious caregivers choose to allot time, energy, and compassion to themselves as well as their care recipients. You believe taking care of yourself physically, emotionally, and spiritually greatly benefits both you and your care recipient. In fact, caregiving quality improves when you care enough about yourself to take time out from caregiving for activities that make *you* happier and more refreshed.

Through the use of mindfulness and self-care techniques, which we'll discuss a bit later, you keep the focus on yourself as a whole person, and are not wrapped up solely in your caregiving role. You acknowledge and honor the fact that you are still a daughter, son, spouse, parent, grandparent, niece, nephew, friend, neighbor, and/or coworker. As a self-aware, conscious caregiver, you serve the entirety of your needs as a person while simultaneously acting as a loving caregiver.

This self-awareness grows when you take time to pause mindfully and notice your immediate situation instead of racing nonstop through your day trying to get everything done. Then, when you reflect upon what you're seeing without judgment or attaching labels, more (and often kinder or more logical) options for decisions and challenges will result. This brief oasis in time and space gives conscious caregivers breathing room to notice details and fully experience the moment they're in.

You pause, observe, reflect on your options, and then act. This mindfulness thinking pattern can be applied to your interactions with your care recipient, your family caregiving team, and health professionals caring for your loved one. As you learn this way of thinking and responding, caregiving stress will decrease, and you will likely find yourself using these techniques in other life situations too.

CONSCIOUS CONNECTIONS

According to *Caregiving in the U.S. 2015*, a large majority of caregivers (85 percent) provide care for a relative, with 49 percent caring for a parent or parent-in-law. Ten percent provide care for a spouse—logging a staggering 44.6 caregiving hours per week while doing so. In comparison, family members average 24.4 hours a week providing care for other loved ones, and nearly 25 percent provide 41 or more hours of care a week.

One thing about caregiving that remains constant is that *your role will change* over time. Your loved one will continue aging, or new health issues might arise and she will likely need increased assistance. That's why there is not a single "formula" for being an expert family caregiver.

Each caregiving journey is unique and unpredictable. As a result, your creative problem-solving skills will be engaged as long as you are a caregiver. No matter how much your role changes during caregiving, you have this inner constant to rely on—a conscious caregiver's perspective.

Caregiving is definitely challenging, exhausting, and heartbreaking, but it's also filled with beautiful, intimate moments to cherish. As difficult as it is to see a loved one decline, family caregivers also experience tenderness, gratitude, devotion, patience, and love. During the most difficult times, when you are stressed to the maximum, you are still surrounded by a beautiful world to acknowledge and be grateful for every day. Conscious caregivers learn how to search within themselves to find and appreciate this positive attitude, and one way you'll learn how to do this is by being mindful.

Be Mindful

Conscious caregiving begins with mindfulness, the ancient art of practicing self-awareness in the present moment without judgment. It means pausing in the midst of any situation and taking time to pay attention to yourself, your environment, and the overall situation. You don't try to control, assess, or judge. You become aware of the here and now. Mindfulness asks that you pause, observe, and reflect, and then act or respond. This could happen in seconds or over a longer period of time depending upon the situation.

The first step in mindfulness is to pause, stop all talking and actions, and become focused on the present. Stop showering your loved one, stop racing from task to task, stop thinking of what's next on your caregiving to-do list, and stop reliving prior events of the day or week in your head. Instead, ask yourself what is happening at this very moment in front of your eyes. For example, if you're showering your loved one, pause and quietly observe the shower scene before you. Stop lathering, hair washing, or rinsing off your loved one. Stop talking. View what's before you as if you're watching a movie.

The next step in mindfulness is paying attention. Deliberately take in your immediate surroundings, both physical and emotional. Use your senses to notice what space you are in, what the noise level is, and how the environment makes you feel. Are you in your parents' home or at a doctor's appointment with one of them, taking a walk around your town, or in a crowded store in a mall? Is it well lit or dim? Is there background noise, such as birds chirping, a TV blaring, or peaceful music playing?

How do you feel in this space? What does your body (inside and out) sense at this very moment? Are your muscles tense or relaxed? Do you have a headache? Are you smiling or frowning? What are your emotions? Are you enjoying yourself? Feeling relaxed? Are you annoyed or upset? Are you feeling guilty? Frustrated? Anxious? Unsure of yourself? Notice what surrounds you in every way possible via your five senses.

Once you have your input, neither criticize nor praise what you observe. This is one of the hardest parts of mindfulness. Do not label yourself, your loved one, or anyone else with you. Be aware, open-minded, and respectful of whatever you're experiencing. Your brain is constantly assessing and chattering internally based upon these assessments. Shut off your internal dialogue. Do your best not to judge; simply absorb what's immediately around you. Remember the phrase, "It is what it is." Be a nonjudgmental self-reporter.

By pushing the pause button on your busy day in these ways, you immediately create a small space of calmness as you focus on the moment. In this quiet space, you can catch your breath during a hectic day, assess your state of being, and use this time to change your thoughts, attitudes, or actions if needed. By checking in with yourself, you can decide if you need a longer interval of peace and make that happen—either immediately or via a break later in the day—to give yourself some much-needed time, attention, and self-care. Ultimately the goal is to incorporate this inner calm throughout other parts of your day. Through mindfulness you will realize you have the power to take charge of how you view any situation, and even more importantly, how you may respond to it.

Being present in a moment of caregiving can also help you sense the richness and beauty in the experience. When you're focused on and engaging mindfully with your loved one, you'll notice things you might ordinarily miss if you're in a hurry or distracted. How beautifully soft and smooth your mother's hands are even at her advanced age. Your father's eyes crinkling at the corners when he gives his hearty chuckle. Hearing that sweet story your aunt tells about how she and your uncle met in high school. These are conscious caregiver treasures you don't want to miss.

CASE STUDY: Adrian and Mindfulness

Taking just a few minutes to be mindful and start your day right will help you be prepared to meet whatever challenges lie ahead.

Adrian wakes up at six a.m. to her alarm clock blaring. Immediately she jumps out of bed and, as she dresses, begins thinking of everything she needs to accomplish that day, at work and for her family, plus spending time with her mom in the hospital, where she is recuperating from surgery. She quickly makes breakfast for herself and her two teenagers, but they don't have time to enjoy eating together because the kids are running late. The teens each grab an energy bar and a banana as they rush out the door to school. Her husband left even earlier for a breakfast work meeting before she got up. After being awake for only 60 minutes, Adrian can already feel the tension in her body and dreads the rest of the day ahead.

Instead of continuing down this stressful path, Adrian decides to use some mindfulness techniques to reset her day. First, she turns off the TV and notices the sounds of birds chirping in their backyard. Then she decides to finish her breakfast slowly, enjoy her tea, and read a magazine article she'd put aside to return to when she had time. Just these few extra minutes of peace, indulging in a few things she enjoys, create a shift in her mood and attitude. Afterward, she is ready to tackle the rest of her day in a more cheerful and relaxed state. Yes, it might take a few extra, unplanned-for minutes out of her day, but the positive, long-term effects are worth the small amount of time Adrian spends to make this shift happen.

> "One person caring about another represents life's greatest value."
>
> —Jim Rohn, American author and motivational speaker

TAKING ON NEW RESPONSIBILITIES

The responsibilities that you'll take on as a caregiver will vary depending upon your care recipient's living situation and health status. On any given day exact steps to take and tasks to accomplish will be different for every family caregiver. You will likely find yourself doing things you never thought you could or would do for your loved ones. This may be something logistical, such as driving them around on errands, or something more intimate, such as bathing them and changing their diapers. You may be surprised by what is asked of you and by how you respond to these new roles. When faced with a new caregiving task you'd rather not do, as a conscious caregiver, you'll respond calmly instead of becoming upset by it. By using mindfulness techniques to pause, observe, reflect, and respond, you will decide how to complete the job yourself or think of smart, alternate ways to accomplish it.

Changing Responsibilities

Caregiving can be compared to parenting in this way: the status quo usually doesn't last very long. Just when you think you have your loved one's daily needs under control, something will change, and you'll need to figure out new, creative responses to different challenges.

For example, most toddlers take a daily afternoon nap. As a parent, it was wonderful getting that one- to two-hour break, either to indulge in a relaxing activity or accomplish other chores while your little one was sleeping. As time went on, it became more and more difficult to get your child down for a nap; then that precious free time you so looked forward to daily was shortened and eventually gone completely. What did you do to remedy this? Many parents create an enforced "quiet time," where their child plays quietly in his or her room instead of napping—a win-win for parent and child.

The transition from a daily naptime to the creation of quiet time happens little by little, until the parent and child are both able to accept the changes and adjust. Slow and gradual changes in routines should be implemented in caregiving situations as well, in order to allow your loved one to retain his or her dignity and independence for as long as possible. The same will likely be true for you and your loved one, as you'll see in the following case study.

CASE STUDY: Tony and New Solutions

Tony's father, Joseph, lives in a condominium in a senior living community not far from Tony's home. Joseph, age eighty-nine, is still active and mentally sharp but becoming frailer physically. The community's laundry facilities are a short walk from Joseph's condominium, where he's been doing his laundry independently since his wife passed away a few years ago. Noticing his father was slowing down, Tony shifted the laundry routine over time. First, he bought Joseph a laundry basket on wheels to transport the laundry back and forth. Then, Tony visited on laundry day and helped Joseph do his laundry. And finally, Tony took Joseph's laundry home to do with his, bringing it back folded or on hangers, all ready to wear.

Creative problem-solving was put into practice as Joseph needed more assistance. Tony's decision to make changes gradually made it easier for Joseph to preserve his dignity and accept this help. If Tony had taken over doing his father's laundry completely as the first solution, Joseph might have felt hurt and insulted having his independence disregarded. Making transitions in baby steps whenever possible is an easier and kinder route to the goal. Allow your loved ones to keep their independence and dignity. Let them do as much as they can for as long as they can, as long as it is safe for them to do so.

THE IMPACT OF ROLE CONFUSION

The way you take care of and identify with your loved one can and likely will change over the course of the caregiving journey that you'll share. This can lead to a sense of role confusion, where you feel uncertain about how to relate to and interact with him. Are you still his spouse or child, or do you feel like his parent now?

The relationship you have with your care recipient (parent, spouse, partner, extended family member, or friend) has existed and developed over a long period of time. Then, either suddenly or in small steps, your loved one declined and you found yourself in the role of caregiver, which was likely confusing for everyone involved. It can be difficult for you to separate your role of caregiver from your previous role of spouse, child, niece, nephew, grandchild, or friend. And your care recipient may object to her new role as someone less than 100 percent independent, feel insulted, and initially decline your offers of help.

Caregiving for a parent is often called "role reversal," meaning you become a parent to your parent. But it isn't a complete role reversal in every sense. She will always be your parent and you will remain her child. The relationship dynamics might change now, but you can't erase the many years your parent spent raising you and all that you've experienced together as a family.

And, unlike in a parent-child relationship, you do not have legal responsibility for your parent. You cannot "tell her what to do" like you would a child. (That is, unless her decline causes specific durable powers of attorney to be exercised, such as in the case of dementia or Alzheimer's disease.)

When a spouse declines, role confusion has an additional, practical dimension. You now have the extra responsibilities your spouse handled until she could no longer do them. These could range from taking out garbage cans on trash day to being wholly in charge of your family's finances and investments. You might enjoy doing some of these chores and dislike others, but your to-do list definitely grows longer.

It's important for you to keep in mind that, although the job of caregiving has affected you and your life, it has also greatly affected your loved one. Make a conscious attempt to remember that your care recipient is in a new life stage in which she is experiencing many losses, such as the loss of health, mobility, strength, and independence. She is likely struggling with issues around self-image, self-respect, and emotions, such as sadness, frustration, fear, and anger. Be sensitive and respectful of your loved one's feelings, honor her wishes, and uphold her dignity as you help to navigate through these changes and those ahead.

That said, it's important that you recognize and identify the varying emotions that you're experiencing as a caregiver as well.

CONSCIOUS CONNECTIONS

According to the Social Security Administration, a man who is sixty-five years old today can expect to live on average to age eighty-four, and a woman of sixty-five today should live to age eighty-six. And these are just averages. About one of every four people in this older adult demographic today will live past age ninety, and one out of ten will live past age ninety-five. With more people living longer, two things are certain: more older adults will decline physically and cognitively, and more conscious caregivers will be needed to care for them.

UNDERSTANDING YOUR EMOTIONS

Throughout your caregiving journey you will experience a range of emotions—joy, satisfaction, love, gratitude, sadness, fear, guilt, anger, frustration, depression, confusion, impatience, stress, grief, exhaustion, and more. Some of these contrasting feelings can occur within minutes of each other and drain you of energy.

Do you feel alone or isolated in your caregiving role? Do you think, *No one understands what I'm going through*? Many caregivers feel this way. After all, it's very hard, and can be heartbreaking, seeing a loved one decline. First, recognize you are not alone and are experiencing normal emotions all family caregivers feel. Second, be proud of yourself for facing a difficult situation and staying by your loved one's side. Even if you're a long-distance caregiver, "being there" by phone or online makes a huge difference. Some people run away from caring for aging relatives, but you haven't. Kudos for that. Third, recognize that your caregiving role will not last forever, which is both a positive and a negative.

Some emotions you may find yourself struggling with include:

Caregiving Guilt

Caregivers live with constant guilt. Guilt that you're not doing a good enough job. Guilt when you take a well-deserved break and aren't there, whether for a few minutes, days, or weeks. Guilt when you resent your role and even dislike your care recipient at times.

Caregiving is one of the most challenging roles you'll ever take on, and as a conscious caregiver you understand the need to slow down and recognize the guilty feelings you're having. Give yourself permission to feel these negative feelings, but also try to limit them. It's okay to have a "pity party" daily if needed, but let it last only five to ten minutes, then put those feelings on the back burner, and choose to continue your day with an improved, more optimistic attitude. As a conscious caregiver, you know it's okay to validate the full range of your experiences, be compassionate toward yourself, and take care of yourself. Remember, you can't pour from an empty cup, so be sure to keep your reserves filled. It's similar to traveling on an airplane, when the flight attendant instructs you to put on your oxygen mask first before you put on your child's. You need to operate from a position of strength, and taking care of yourself first is the way to accomplish that.

EXERCISE:
Use Mindfulness to Identify Your Emotions

Mindfulness is the ancient art of practicing self-awareness in the present moment without judgment. It means pausing at any moment and taking time to pay attention to yourself, your environment, and the overall situation. You don't try to control, assess, or judge. You are simply aware of the here and now, including your deepest, darkest feelings. Caregivers often have trouble identifying and dealing with their negative feelings in particular, so take a mindful approach and try the following:

Choose a place and time to be alone and think about your feelings without interruptions or distractions. Write down your deepest feelings *for your eyes only*. Let out all of your confusion, worries, and fears in a personal journal, knowing no one but you will ever read it. Don't edit yourself; write whatever you really feel. (It's fine to include positive feelings in your journal, too, but negative ones are best served in this exercise.) Another way to do this is by writing a letter to your care recipient with your negative emotions unleashed that you never send.

Putting your feelings into words through writing helps you reach a place of peace internally because you release the intensity of those painful emotions you're experiencing. You can also clarify exactly what is troubling you and perhaps gain insight into your care recipient's perspective as you write. If you're venting about a specific problem, writing can unlock creative and intuitive abilities, which can lead to solutions you didn't see before.

Resentment

As a caregiver, you'll likely find yourself feeling resentment at some point. This is a totally normal emotion under the circumstances, and it should be acknowledged. It's true that your life has been hijacked to some degree by these new responsibilities, and is not 100 percent under your control. It's not fun having to miss your friend's Super Bowl party at the last minute because you need to stay home with your father, who needs care. Yes, you feel like dodging your spouse's call when you're out running errands and taking a brief caregiving breather. And it's definitely a drag to spend days at the hospital with your loved one as he recuperates from surgery.

Feeling resentment wastes emotional and mental energy on something that probably can't be changed right away. But you *can* still be an excellent caregiver even though you feel negative emotions at times.

In order to alleviate the resentment, try using the previous writing exercise to vent about those feelings. Also, keep in mind that caregiving is temporary: the scenario is sure to change, and someday you will no longer be a caregiver. Try to change your attitude and cherish this bonus time with your loved one, because not everyone gets the opportunity to experience it.

And do your best to separate resentment of your caregiving role from bad feelings toward your care recipient. Yes, you might feel caregiving is a burden sometimes, but chances are you don't really dislike your loved one. If you weren't concerned about his welfare, you'd walk away, which you haven't done. So hang in there. This too shall pass.

Fear of the Future

Fear of the future and how you will deal with it is another major caregiving emotion. You begin to worry about what the future will be like for yourself and your loved one. Will he experience pain? How will you juggle your caregiving, family, and/or work responsibilities? Do you have enough money saved to cover medical expenses? And more ...

You can find relief from many of your fears through education. Do research and read everything you can about your care recipient's diagnosis, if there is one. Meet with his doctor(s) and nurses as well as people in organizations dedicated to research or finding a cure for the disease (for example, the American Heart Association) to ask questions. Consult an elder-law attorney and/or financial planner if your loved one's financial affairs are not in order. Find a support group for caregivers or one centered around the disease to gather more information from others going through similar scenarios. Taking actions, even small ones, will move you from an emotional state of mind to a fact-gathering, intellectual one. The adage "Knowledge is power" rings true for family caregivers. And while the act of gathering information and resources won't change your loved one's diagnosis or decline, knowledge will lead you to more clarity about what the future will hold. This knowledge will allow you to prepare for and adjust in a calmer way to the changes as they come.

Grief

Grief is another common emotion experienced by caregivers. You may initially think this sounds silly. After all, your loved one is still alive. How can you grieve for someone who you're spending so much time with and energy on?

Think of it this way: even while your loved one is alive, you're grieving the loss of the person he once was, especially if he has a progressive illness, like Alzheimer's disease. As a loved one needs increased assistance, you feel a sense of loss—the loss of his capabilities and independence, the loss of the chance to complete future plans, or the loss of your companion to share things with if you're caring for your spouse. Grief, which is discussed in more detail in Chapters 9 and 10, is usually associated with death, but anticipatory grief starts when you experience these losses even before your loved one passes away.

Identify and accept anticipatory grief as normal. Speak about the losses you're experiencing with a trusted friend, family member, or clergy person. Writing about your feelings in a journal is often beneficial. Support group co-members are probably also feeling grief and loss, so bring up the topic for discussion. Most importantly, get your feelings out in whatever manner works best for you. After all, taking care of yourself alongside your loved one is part of what conscious caregiving is all about!

One way to deal with this grief, especially if your loved one has a life-threatening or progressive disease, such as Alzheimer's, is to establish a "new" relationship as his abilities change. The arts, especially music, are a wonderful way to connect with your loved one. Play his favorite music and sing along together when possible. Even when my mother couldn't walk or speak during the late stages of Alzheimer's disease, when she heard her favorite songs playing, she would smile and gently nod her head up and down. She also loved gardening her whole life, so I bought a large coffee-table book of beautiful flower photography that we'd look through together during visits. She would hold the book in her lap and gently caress the pages, which I believe was her nonverbal way of expressing her great enjoyment of this two-dimensional garden.

CHAPTER SUMMARY

The following are takeaways, action steps, and reminders to help your caregiving journey progress smoothly.

- Conscious caregivers choose to give time, energy, and compassion to themselves as well as their care recipients. They use mindfulness and self-care techniques to care for themselves physically, emotionally, and spiritually. Through increased self-awareness, a conscious caregiver more easily finds and appreciates the beautiful moments the journey holds. In any situation remember to pause, observe, and reflect, and then respond or act.
- There are both positive and negative aspects to being a family caregiver. You will experience joy, sadness, exhaustion, gratitude, love, angst, and more. The one constant is that your role will keep changing as your loved one declines. And your experience as a caregiver will not last forever, unfortunately.
- You will wear a variety of hats as a caregiver, sometimes several different ones all within one day. No matter what roles you take on daily, your care recipient's safety must be your number one priority. This is followed by meeting her basic needs of shelter, nutritious food, and medical care.
- You will learn about your strengths through this life experience. You will find creativity and problem-solving skills you may not have realized you possess. You will also wrestle with negative emotions, such as fear and grief, and learn how to control them through mindfulness.
- Most caregivers and their care recipients experience a degree of role confusion. Sometimes it's hard to find the place where being an adult child ends and being a family caregiver begins. Your loved one is also adjusting to his diminished capabilities and may initially greatly resent and reject your help.

CHAPTER 2

Caregiver Stress and Burnout

Now that you know what conscious caregiving is and how you may be feeling about your new role and the new relationship dynamic between you and your loved one, let's take a look at why paying attention to those emotions is crucial to being a great caregiver.

Do you ever feel so exhausted when you wake up that you simply can't, or don't want to, get out of bed? Do you find that little things that usually don't bother you are making you angry? Are you snapping at your loved one? Do you have trouble sleeping? Are you spending less time with friends? Are you getting sick more often? Have you been feeling down in the dumps? If so, you could be approaching caregiver burnout. In this chapter you'll learn how to look for the signs of burnout, alleviate stress, and avoid slipping into burnout.

WHAT IS CAREGIVER BURNOUT?

Caregiver burnout occurs when you find yourself in a state of physical, emotional, and mental exhaustion. You may sense a change in your overall attitude, from being caring and positive to feeling negative or unconcerned about your world and those in it.

Some stress in life is a positive thing because it encourages you to meet challenges and find solutions. And stress can't be avoided completely while caregiving. But high levels of stress over a long period of caregiving (or even over a shorter but more intense time span) can lead to caregiver burnout. Family caregivers are either with their loved ones or "on call" for them daily, often for months at a time. Sometimes your loved one's physical or emotional needs may overwhelm you. You feel like you're always giving—to your care recipient, your immediate family, your work, and your friends. You wonder if there's any time or energy left over for you.

Caregiver Burnout and Health Risks

High levels of chronic stress can degrade your health and harm your relationship with your loved one. The report *Caregiving in the U.S. 2015* shows that four in ten caregivers consider their caregiving situations to be highly stressful, and the toll on a caregiver's health increases over time. Also, those caring for a close relative, such as a spouse or parent, are at a much greater risk of declining health than those caring for another relative or non-relative.

Long-term stress of any kind, including caregiver stress, can lead to serious health problems if left unchecked. When you are stressed, any problem you encounter feels magnified tenfold in your mind, and seeking care for any of your existing or new health conditions can seem impossible to do. However, this is a critical time to care for yourself because caregiver stress and burnout can worsen or increase the risk of many health problems, such as:

- A weakened immune system, which can lead to more illnesses and longer recovery time after surgery and other medical procedures
- Higher levels of anxiety and depression
- Higher risk of chronic diseases, such as stroke, heart disease, cancer, type 2 diabetes, and arthritis
- Obesity
- Digestion problems
- Headaches

- Body aches and pains
- Substance abuse

If you are experiencing any of these health issues, see your doctor as soon as possible. Mention that you think the conditions are caused or being exacerbated by caregiving, and ask for help.

Caregiver Burnout's Effect on Your Life

Along with these serious health issues, caregiver burnout can hurt your ability to function on a regular basis. How do you get through the day when you're on an emotional roller coaster—feeling angry one minute and helpless the next? It's hard to get through the daily caregiving routine with your loved one if you're feeling alone or that no one understands what you're going through. Stress and burnout can make it difficult for you to make decisions or even think clearly. And your spouse, children, and friends may be getting tired of always being put last in favor of your care recipient and/or work responsibilities.

Accept that you wouldn't be human if you didn't experience some degree of stress. No one in your situation can remain strong and function at the top of their abilities all the time. Stress might occur as a brief episode lasting only a few hours or days, or it may last longer, becoming increasingly intense. The key is to recognize the symptoms early on and take steps to prevent the problem from worsening.

CASE STUDY: Beth and Caregiver Burnout

Beth, age sixty-four, cared for her husband, Sheldon, for eight years before he succumbed to end-stage renal disease at age sixty-nine. He was on dialysis during the last five years of his life. The most difficult aspect of caregiving for Beth was losing the "normal" way of life they previously had. Everything revolved around his illness. When Sheldon became weaker and even walking to the car became difficult, they stopped going out to plays and concerts, which they used to enjoy regularly, and Beth planned very few social engagements. She felt guilty sometimes because she could still do whatever she wanted while Sheldon couldn't. And she felt angry because she felt robbed of the life she was missing.

She says, "With each passing year of his illness, there were fewer and fewer moments of peace. The simplest things became difficult as the disease progressed. I felt invisible and powerless as it eclipsed our lives. The best way I can describe it was that I was married to two entities—Sheldon and kidney disease." Her full-time teaching job became a welcome escape from the stress she felt at home. She would cry on her drive to school, then pull it together as she walked in. And spending every Saturday with their grandson provided her with great joy. Her sister-in-law, who lived in another state, was available by phone, so Beth "would share [her] fears, anxiety, and anger over the negative changes with her."

SIGNS TO LOOK FOR

Many caregivers don't recognize when they are approaching burnout because they are so focused on their care recipient's needs and ignore their own state of being. Making self-awareness part of your practice of conscious caregiving is the first step in avoiding caregiver stress and burnout. Use mindfulness as your tool to pause and become aware of how you are functioning and do a self-assessment. Begin with the following exercise to see how you are managing overall on a daily basis.

EXERCISE: Are You Experiencing Caregiver Burnout?

Here are more questions to help you decide if you are approaching, or may already be experiencing, caregiver burnout. Answer them honestly. Your health and well-being depend on your self-analysis—and your health directly affects your care recipient's life.

- Have your sleep patterns changed? Do you have trouble falling asleep, wake up multiple times during the night, or feel exhausted upon awakening?
- Do you feel worried or anxious?
- Do you feel constantly irritated? Are things upsetting you that didn't before?
- Do you find yourself speaking sharply to your care recipient or family?
- Do you feel resentment toward your care recipient or other family members?
- Are you less social and more isolated? Are you avoiding social activities you used to enjoy?
- Do you frequently yell, cry, or feel angry?
- Do you feel overwhelmed?
- Have you stopped exercising?
- Have you started or increased unhealthy behaviors, such as drinking too much alcohol, taking drugs, or smoking tobacco or marijuana?
- Do you feel tired most of the day?
- Are you having conflicts with other family members or friends?
- Have you had trouble keeping your mind focused or difficulty concentrating?
- Has it been harder to make decisions?

- Do you feel a loss of privacy and/or personal time?
- Do you feel torn between caregiving, work, and family responsibilities?
- Do you feel alone?
- Have you been ill with a headache, stomach ailment, or cold? Do you feel aches or pain anywhere?
- Are you putting off necessary physical checkups?
- Are you taking medications, vitamins, and supplements as prescribed?
- Have your appetite and/or weight changed?
- Do you have thoughts about wanting to hurt yourself or your care recipient? (If so, call 911 and/or the National Suicide Prevention Lifeline at 1-800-273-8255 immediately.)
- Has anyone suggested to you that you are burning out?

If you've identified any of these signs, the mindfulness practices discussed in this and the following chapter can prevent them from getting worse.

HOW TO AVOID CAREGIVER BURNOUT

It's hard as a caregiver to admit when you're feeling angry, frustrated, tired, and/or overwhelmed, but burnout can sneak up on you. It usually doesn't happen overnight; it begins with one or two symptoms, then progresses. If you've identified some symptoms of caregiver burnout, don't worry. An important step toward being a conscious caregiver is recognizing your current state of being. Then you can figure out ways that will work for you to alleviate the pressure. The following sections outline steps you can take, both immediately and long term, to lower your stress level.

Accept Help

When you were parenting your children, you didn't handle all of the childrearing responsibilities alone. During that stage of life, you created a "village," relying in part on immediate and extended family, friends, neighbors, teachers, coaches, after-school programs, and babysitters for help. Now is another time in your life to create a circle of support. If you try to do everything on your own, you risk burning out.

Family caregivers often have a blind spot when it comes to their own needs and accepting help from others. It's not a sign of weakness to need or accept help. In fact, it's actually a sign of self-knowledge and wisdom. Accept the reality that no one can be an effective caregiver alone. It truly "takes a village" to care for someone, so begin asking for help in specific ways. Yes, you are the primary caregiver, but there are many ways siblings or friends can assist you, even from afar. Do some brainstorming first about who you know and what their strengths are. Your sister is great with numbers? Suggest she take over the financial aspects of your loved one's care—paying bills, reconciling bank statements, managing investments, etc. Do you have a neighbor who loves to organize? Allow her to go through your parent's or spouse's garage, pantry, or any closets that you don't have the time or energy to tackle. Do you have a child who enjoys gardening? Let him take over watering the plants, mowing the lawn, trimming the bushes, or sweeping the patio.

"You can do anything, but not everything."

—David Allen, management and productivity consultant

People will often ask, "How can I help?" Do your best to analyze what your caregiving needs are ahead of time, large and small, and write them all down. Do you need help with grocery shopping or errands? Do you need research done about local care facilities? Do you need someone to keep your loved one company while you take a break? Update the list every week or even more frequently because circumstances can change quickly. By making a list, you will be ready to give out specific assignments whenever family or friends ask to help. Be prepared with a list of specific answers they can choose from and then accept the help graciously.

CASE STUDY: Colleen and Caregiver Burnout

Colleen, a caregiving daughter who moved back into her childhood home with her father when he became ill, used a weekly email to communicate with her "team" and give assignments.

She says, "People wanted to help, but they didn't know how. So I developed a once-a-week email where I would provide an update on what happened during the week and how he was doing. I would write a brief story, make it humorous, and put some photos in it. Then I also made research assignments. For example, I'd tell my sister-in-law, 'Research grippy socks for adults.' Then she would research them, order the best ones for Dad online, and have ten pairs delivered to his house. I gave someone else the assignment to research surgery possibilities. Making these assignments within the weekly email worked out great because people felt good that they could do something that was enormously helpful."

Colleen found a streamlined way to keep her concerned family members and friends updated while doling out specific assignments to help her accomplish needed tasks. This allowed her to remain in better spirits overall because she knew she had other people helping her. It's never too soon to ask for help. Almost every family caregiver I speak with says they wish they'd asked for help sooner than they did.

Learn to Delegate

After you assign a task, move on to something else. Give those helping you a chance to do the best job they can. Don't hover over them or make them feel inadequate—that's wasted time and energy on your part. Unless it's a matter of safety, does it really matter if your helper doesn't do the task the exact same way, or up to your high standard, as long as it gets done? Use a mindfulness technique to locate your thought process, stop micromanaging your helper, and move on. After the task is completed, be sure to thank your helper and have your loved one do so too, if possible. Do your utmost not to criticize helpers' efforts so they will be willing to help again.

Use Respite Care

Taking care of a loved one can be physically and emotionally draining. Yet family caregivers are indispensable . . . or at least they think they are. "No one can take care of my loved one the way I do" is a statement family caregivers often say aloud or secretly believe. And it is correct in certain ways. You *do* have a unique relationship with your care recipient, one that can never be duplicated exactly. But so do their siblings, other adult children, grandchildren, cousins, other family, and friends. Don't get caught up in the mistaken belief you are the only one who can give care, because it stops you from allowing others to provide *you* with a much-needed break.

Letting others help you will give you time to take care of yourself, alleviate stress, and prevent you from slipping into burnout. Respite care services provide you with a temporary rest from caregiving through a variety of options while your loved one continues to receive the care she needs. This break (or respite) could be several hours each week to run personal errands or a vacation lasting as long as you wish. Ironically, taking time away from your care recipient could lead to your loved one aging in place longer, because you will be calmer, less stressed, and in better physical health. Interpersonal relationships with your loved one and others will turn more positive. Taking care of your own needs increases your ability to provide sustained, higher-quality care.

Add Care at Home

If you feel reluctant to take this step, turn to a friend or family member as a helper. Have your "reliever" first visit when you and your loved one normally spend time together. Arrange several visits before you take time away, so your helper can get to know your care recipient's typical routines, likes and dislikes, etc. This will also give your care recipient time to get accustomed to other people assisting him, rather than having this change occur suddenly on the actual day you'll be gone. Your loved one will reap the added benefits of socializing with different people too.

Begin slowly. After this "orientation" period, spend only two to four hours away initially. Once you see that all is going well, you will feel more comfortable increasing the time you're away from your loved one. It's wise to have several relievers to call on for assistance as backup on different days or for different lengths of time. Let your care recipient provide input and feedback as to who best helps, and for what periods of time to schedule regular, ongoing respite care at home.

Hiring in-home, non-medical care (or skilled nursing care, if needed) through a state-licensed agency is another way to arrange for some precious time off.

An agency should send several candidates for you and your loved one to interview and select from. Don't hesitate to try new helpers until you and your loved one are satisfied with your choice, and again, begin with short time increments. It's also a good idea to have more than one paid caregiver on your "favorites" list as backup just as you have on your family and friends helper list.

CONSCIOUS CONNECTIONS

If you're looking to hire in-home care, contact your local Area Agency on Aging (AAA) by phone or online for referrals to agencies. Or do an online search on the Department of Health and Human Services' Eldercare Locator at www.eldercare.gov. Ask neighbors or friends in your area for referrals to licensed agencies they've found helpful.

Use Adult Day Services

Ask at local senior centers, your church or temple, or your doctor's office or do an online search to see if your community has adult day services as another win-win choice for you and your care recipient. Adult day centers are run by professional care staff for adults who need assistance or supervision on weekdays. A center may be located in its own building or in a senior center, church, skilled nursing facility, hospital, or school. These comprehensive programs provide social interaction, meals and snacks, a wide range of activities, exercise, and some health care services. Older adults with physical disabilities and/or cognitive impairments, who are frail, or feel bored at home are all candidates to attend this type of day program. Your care recipient will look forward to going to a safe and friendly environment while you enjoy some time off. Adult day centers also offer family support groups, workshops, and referrals to other community services.

There is another type of program called adult day *health* services. This medical model offers intensive health, therapeutic, and social services for seniors with serious medical conditions and those at risk of requiring nursing home care.

Not all states have adult day programs. If they are offered in your community, visit and observe those closest to you. Speak with the staff and ask to contact families whose loved ones currently attend the programs as references. Costs vary depending upon location, number of days attending, and services offered, but most are private pay and not covered by Medicare insurance. Some financial assistance may be available through a federal or state program, such as the Department of Veterans Affairs (VA).

Use Respite Care in an Eldercare Facility

A respite stay for your loved one in an assisted living or smaller, six-bed residential care community is another choice. Respite care is usually short-term, typically lasting from one week to one month maximum in a community that provides housing, care, activities, and supervision. It's a choice to consider when you have to travel for business or want to take a vacation. You might use respite care when your loved one's home needs repairs or remodeling, or, if she is living with you, during any messy home improvement projects you have to do. If your loved one lives alone, you might arrange respite care after surgery as a chance to regain her strength or mobility following a stay at a rehabilitation facility and before returning home. Identify and visit several eldercare facilities that offer respite care in advance, if possible, so you will know which one your family prefers to use, whether as planned or in an emergency.

CONSCIOUS CONNECTIONS

Sixty percent of caregivers report that they are working while caregiving, with 56 percent employed full-time, according to *Caregiving in the U.S. 2015*. Nearly half of family caregivers provide care to someone age seventy-five or older. Most have been in their role for an average of four years, and only about half (53 percent) say another unpaid caregiver helps their care recipient. One in three caregivers have no help at all—paid or unpaid. When asked if they had a choice taking on their caregiving role, half of the respondents replied no.

Take Time Off from Work

If you're working, you are juggling two full-time jobs—your career and caregiving. Cutting back on your workday, at least in part, may be an option worth exploring. You will always be able to do more work, but your loved one's lifetime is limited. If you continue on the nonstop treadmill of career and caregiving, something's going to give out, and it will most likely be you.

More and more companies are aware of, and sympathetic to, the needs of employees with aging loved ones. Ask your employer to work with you to devise a backup plan to cover your workload should you need to leave due to an emergency, both in the short term and in cases where you'll need to be away from work for a longer time period.

Explore the possibilities of telecommuting or taking a leave of absence under the Family and Medical Leave Act. This law requires employers with fifty or more employees to provide up to twelve weeks of unpaid, job-protected leave for people who need time off to care for a seriously ill family member. Some companies offer additional eldercare benefits, such as family caregiving workshops and referrals to local eldercare services. Check with your company's human resources department to learn about your options.

Join a Support Group

Joining a support group combats isolation you may experience, physically and emotionally. Support group members who connect at meetings often become friends. Members who live in close proximity may start carpooling to meetings, go out for coffee or a meal afterward to continue the discussions, and/or get together at other times simply to socialize. Some form a "respite cooperative," so a caregiver-friend can have a break to get out while a trusted friend is staying with his or her loved one.

It's wise to "shop" for a support group you feel comfortable with. This includes analyzing everything about it—from the physical setting and the member demographics to the leader's style and the meeting format. There is most likely a support group that is the right fit for you, so try different groups until you find it.

On the other hand, have patience while looking. Attend at least two meetings of a group before crossing it off of your list. You want to be sure your first impression was valid, even if it wasn't necessarily a positive one. What's an extra hour out of your life when it could lead to a positive long-term experience? Some caregivers find they enjoy going to multiple support groups regularly because each one offers something different—another acceptable strategy that support group leaders themselves endorse.

Don't feel you must attend every meeting to get value from the group. If you don't have a pressing need or questions, it's okay to skip a meeting and return again when you feel it would be beneficial.

Online support groups are readily available 24/7 and easy to join due to technology. Use a search engine to find support group meetings based on your location and/or your loved one's diagnosis, or use the search function on *Facebook* to locate and join public or private groups dedicated to your loved one's condition or disease. Communicating and sharing stories with other caregivers from all over the country or world is interesting, helpful, and gratifying. But there is one valuable part of face-to-face relationships with other caregivers that you won't get in any online support group—hugs. And as a caregiver, you can *always* benefit from hugs.

CONSCIOUS CONNECTIONS

Empathy is another reason to join a support group. All of the members, and possibly even the group's leader, are in the midst of caregiving. They truly understand your caregiving ups and downs. The members can steer you to local resources and might also provide firsthand feedback about the various services you're considering, both pros and cons.

Get Organized

Family caregivers experience a continuous learning curve and, as a result, quickly become skilled in planning and problem-solving. Becoming and staying organized is part of both of these skills and leads to diminished stress. And it's not just being organized about your loved one's medications, doctors' appointments, and many other caregiving needs. Applying organizational skills to your work and home life will help you stay more relaxed and composed too. Don't you feel better and have a sense of relief after you've cleaned up your messy desk or cleaned out your refrigerator? These are examples of the calming benefits received from being organized.

Make Lists

If you haven't already been doing so, start making lists. Writing your myriad thoughts on paper rather than having them continuously rattling around in your head will prove extremely calming—both for caregiving and for other personal projects.

EXERCISE: Write It Down

Get those caregiving thoughts out of your head by making a to-do list every night for the following day. This will ensure that you get off to a smoother start in the morning. And you will probably get a better night's sleep because you'll be ready to hit the ground running when you wake up.

Also, if you have an appointment coming up with your loved one's doctor, lawyer, or financial advisor, write down questions as you think of them in the weeks beforehand. That way, you won't leave an appointment and realize that you forgot to ask the question that had been on your mind the week before.

Also, make a list of any clothing (and sizes) or toiletries your loved one needs, and hand the shopping list with some money to the next neighbor or friend who asks to help.

Writing down this information will help you stay organized and will take a lot of the stress out of your day-to-day life with your loved one.

Research Local Support Services

Research local support services to learn what's available. It's best to plan ahead rather than have to hunt for resources during a crisis. Most cities have an Area Agency on Aging (AAA) and/or neighborhood senior centers, which are both good places to begin. Investigate your local senior transportation options, home health care agencies, placement or referral services, Meals on Wheels, elder-law attorneys, social workers, geriatric care managers, geriatricians, assisted living facilities, and other residential care facilities. Get input, arrange visits, and think about and decide which community and medical services your family will use if and when needed. You can avoid greater stress and caregiver burnout if you've created your go-to resource list in advance.

Research Other Caregiving Options Ahead of Time

Start researching other caregiving options for your loved one. It's better to find outside services in advance before they're needed instead of scrambling in an emergency to find alternative care. If your care recipient declines, you may need to hire a professional caregiver to help out at home. Consider the idea of hiring a home health aide to work in your loved one's home for several hours a week as a first step. Then meet with local in-home care or health care agencies to find one you'd enjoy working with when the need arises, if it hasn't already. Know the caregiving burden doesn't have to rest solely on your shoulders indefinitely. Knowing there is assistance ready and waiting for your call will reduce your stress level greatly and help keep burnout at bay. Remember, asking for help is not a sign of weakness but a sign of self-knowledge and wisdom.

CASE STUDY:
Anne and Caregiving Options

Anne's mom, Jeanne, was diagnosed with Alzheimer's disease at only sixty-six years old. Anne's father, Steve, was Jeanne's sole caregiver for about ten years while Anne lent them long-distance support and information through phone calls and visits as often as she could. As Jeanne's disease progressed, she began wandering away from the ranch. As a family they had previously researched senior care facilities near Jeanne and Steve's ranch, as well as others located close to Anne. Initially, Steve thought he would move Jeanne into an assisted living facility near their ranch and eventually they would move closer to Anne. But he learned through the Alzheimer's Association that making only one move versus several moves is easier for Alzheimer's patients. Steve decided to eliminate the extra step and moved Jeanne into dementia care in an assisted living facility near Anne and their extended family while he continued to live independently. For about six months after placing Jeanne, Steve lived with Anne and her husband until he moved into his own apartment, where he lives today.

Moving to a new home and community isn't easy under the best of circumstances, and it's even harder while caring for a loved one. Anne and Steve avoided putting a lot of extra stress on their whole family by doing their homework in advance.

Be Kind to Yourself

A big way to avoid caregiver burnout is to be kind to yourself. You may think that being nice to yourself is weak and self-indulgent, but it's not. When you treat yourself with the same comfort and caring you give others, you shift into a healthier emotional space, feel less anxious and/or depressed, and like yourself more—which are mental states all caregivers need. Be kinder and more patient with yourself in the following ways:

Lower Your Expectations

Remember, you're a human being trying to do what is often a superhuman job. Lower your expectations to focus on the things you have control over, and let go of the rest of the "shoulds."

For example, many caregivers add an additional burden to their caregiving duties by thinking that they are responsible for their loved one's happiness on a daily basis. A family caregiver is responsible for his loved one's safety, attentive medical care, food, and shelter, but this person is *not* required to make the care recipient happy. No one can make another person happy. Offering your loved one ways to continue with interests and hobbies and stay engaged in daily life are reasonable goals to have, but being responsible for his overall happiness is setting an unattainable goal.

Don't Compare

Another way to be kind to yourself is by not comparing yourself with other family caregivers—those within your family-and-friends circle or those you meet in a support group. Each caregiving journey is unique, and every caregiver is too. Due to your life experiences, you have strengths that others do not and vice versa. For example, perhaps you're great at taking your loved one shopping for clothes, and your brother has more patience when speaking with doctors. Don't compare or criticize yourself. Accept that each of you is contributing your strengths.

Are there unrealistic beliefs or expectations you're living your caregiving life by? Think carefully and see what preexisting ideas you may need to change. What can you reasonably get done in one day? Whose help can you enlist? How can you be nicer to yourself?

IF YOU'VE EXPLODED AT A LOVED ONE

Despite your best efforts to prevent it, you may occasionally let out an obvious, irritated sigh, roll your eyes, speak disrespectfully, or even yell at your care recipient. If that happens, put mindfulness into gear. Make a quick exit and have a cooling-off period to give yourself and your loved one time to gain perspective on what just happened. This could be for a few minutes or up to a few days, depending on your caregiving situation.

If you can't leave the situation immediately, at least step out of the room where your care recipient is and do some deep breathing or take a walk until you calm down. Think about what just happened nonjudgmentally. Don't "should" all over yourself, such as thinking "I should be a better son," or "I'm a terrible person." We often hurt the people we love the most. You are human, and no one is perfect. Instead, try the following:

Identify Your Feelings

Try to identify what led up to or triggered these strong emotions and the outburst. After you figure out why, think through constructive options to prevent the anger or frustration from getting out of control again. For example, were you overtired before you got there? Worried about work or other commitments? Could you send another family member to visit or get task XYZ accomplished to ease your mind? If your loved one triggered your emotions about a particular issue, is there a compromise you can offer as a solution?

EXERCISE: Try Role-Playing

If you identify a specific conversation or issue that set you off, try role-playing about that topic with a friend, neighbor, or colleague before you return. This will help you determine how to calmly discuss the issue and interact with your loved one during your next visit. It's best not to involve other family members in this role-playing exercise, because they might have their own emotional bias about the same issue.

Change Your Mode of Contact

If you visit regularly, perhaps you want to touch base via phone several times before another face-to-face visit. Ask someone in your support circle to take on your caregiving duties temporarily during that time. And, if you live with your care recipient, consider calling upon a respite care option, and get away for a little while. By taking a break you'll also afford your loved one time to process what happened.

Repair the Hurt

Before you visit again, resolve to arrive with a pleasant attitude toward your loved one. If you can't visit in a genuinely positive frame of mind, it's probably not time for you to see him again. When you reunite after a blowup, sincerely apologize for whatever you said or did. Show that you are truly sorry in a way that's meaningful to your loved one. Even if you think he in some way helped to create whatever it was that set you off, apologize for your part.

CHAPTER SUMMARY

The following are takeaways, action steps, and reminders to help your caregiving journey progress smoothly.

- Experiencing some stress as a caregiver is normal, but if it increases greatly and/or becomes chronic, you may be experiencing the beginning of caregiver burnout.
- Use mindfulness to become aware of your status. Assess how you are functioning on a day-to-day basis by referring to the list of questions provided.
- Investigate and decide upon respite options so they're ready at your fingertips when needed, rather than waiting until an emergency to first start searching for them. Find family and friend helpers or identify a professional caregiving agency you'll hire from when additional care is needed. See if there are day care respite options your loved one can attend at a local senior center, assisted living community, or church.
- Visit support groups until you find one or more you feel comfortable in. Attend regularly or as needed. They will be a source of ideas, resources, and potential friendships.
- Even the "best" family caregivers can blow their top sometimes. If you do, strategies to repair the hurt could include taking a break from visits, communicating with your loved one in a different way, and/or role-playing with others for solutions to issues. Don't be too hard on or "should" all over yourself—you're human and, therefore, not perfect.

CHAPTER 3

Conscious Caregiving and Self-Care

As you learned in the previous chapter, family caregivers regularly put loved ones and their needs ahead of their own. But in order to stay physically healthy and maintain emotional health, it's important not to lose yourself completely in your caregiving responsibilities. Whether a caregiving journey is short and intense or lasts many years, all family caregivers benefit when they take time out to refresh themselves. Even if you're not approaching caregiver burnout, it's wise to implement ways to relieve the strain and worries that accompany caregiving. It's like cooking with a pressure cooker—better to let out steam in small spurts rather than let it build up and possibly blow the whole lid off the pot.

In this chapter, you'll learn what self-care is, what its benefits are, and how you can start incorporating self-care practices into your daily routine. You may be surprised to learn that you can become a more effective caregiver by *not* being a caregiver sometimes, so let's take a look at how self-care and conscious caregiving go hand in hand.

WHY SELF-CARE?

Family caregivers live very full days. But those days are often overwhelming and riddled with stress, guilt, anger, and anxiety over the care you're giving your loved one. It may seem that your to-do list is never-ending. Maybe you are constantly juggling a full-time career, the needs of your nuclear family, and your daily caregiving responsibilities.

While selflessly giving to others, often for long periods of time, you can lose yourself in the shuffle. And even if putting yourself first goes against your instincts as a caregiver, it is vital to do so. Research shows that medical problems such as physical and mental exhaustion, sleeplessness, depression, and loss of appetite may arise for those who don't take care of themselves. And think about it: If something happens to you, what will your care recipient do? Who will care for your loved one? This is where conscious caregiving becomes so important for both you *and* those who depend on you.

What Is Self-Care?

Self-care is any action that you intentionally take to improve your mental, physical, or emotional health. If you've stopped caring for yourself during your caregiving journey, which is so common, some thoughtful focus can resurrect prior self-care activities and add new ones to your life. It may take a little while to start doing acts of self-care regularly, so begin practicing in small increments. Start with five minutes once a day, increasing self-care to five minutes several times throughout the day, or do it once during the day for a longer period of time. The enjoyable, nourishing activities of your choice will then grow into daily habits you will look forward to indulging in. The time spent on self-care will depend on what you choose to do and your schedule for that particular day.

As a conscious caregiver, you use mindfulness techniques and compassion every day to improve the quality of your care recipient's life. But by spending time focusing on yourself every day, even if only briefly, you will feel better overall and become a calmer, more effective caregiver to your loved one. Keep in mind that, whatever you choose to do, you shouldn't berate yourself too harshly if you fail to find time to relax occasionally. Yes, it's ideal for you to build "me time" into your busy schedule. But don't make fulfilling this goal a new source of stress. That totally defeats the purpose. Everyone is human, and no one is perfect. Forgive yourself, make a plan for the next day, and follow through. And always remember that self-care is not selfish but vital to preventing you from feeling frenzied, exhausted, and overwhelmed.

THE BENEFITS OF SELF-CARE

As I've mentioned, self-care practices are central to your overall health and well-being, and taking these daily steps is proactive and preventive, decreasing your chances of illness as well as caregiver stress and burnout. Self-care leads to a healthier body, a decrease in stress, and improved self-esteem. After all, when you feel better about yourself, it has a positive impact on your interactions with others, including your care recipient. The benefits of self-care are enormous, and include the following:

Improves Physical Health

Many types of active self-care choices can help improve your physical health. Even before you were a caregiver, if you chose something to do that got you up, out, and moving, when you were finished, you felt better—physically and probably also mentally. Our bodies are designed to move, and daily movement is critical to staying fit. When you move, major muscles are engaged, and your body stays tuned up through engaging in a full range of motions. So don't put off playing catch with your grandson or meeting a friend for a quick game of tennis. These types of activities will do you a world of good.

While a healthy body is a fantastic thing on its own, it's also really important when it comes to your role as a conscious caregiver. Why?

Due to better sleep, proper nutrition, and increased energy your caregiving duties will prove less taxing on your body. When you're not distracted or worried about any bodily aches and pains, your mind can focus 100 percent on other important matters.

Improves Sleep Patterns

Because self-care leaves you more relaxed overall, your sleep is likely to improve as well. Going to bed feeling satisfied that you made time to do something for *yourself* as well as your care recipient will also put you in a contented frame of mind, leading to more restful sleep. As a conscious caregiver, achieving restful sleep allows you to be sharper overall during the day and more alert to your care recipient's needs, and it also helps you to problem-solve more easily. It's hard to think clearly when you're feeling tired from reduced or restless sleep.

Reduces and Relieves Stress

By practicing self-care you can lower your stress level and build up your "resilience response" when faced with the challenges that caregiving—and life in general—throws your way. With resilience, the psychological reservoir of strength you call on to carry you through hard times, you confront problems or setbacks head-on and then move forward, sometimes even growing wiser and stronger through the difficulties.

Self-care improves your abilities to face and reduce the physical and emotional stress of caregiving. Adding moments of joy to your day, even in only five-minute increments, reminds you of the many positive things life has to offer when you're not caught up in worrying. When you use mindfulness, instead of continuing to expend energy chaotically, you can slow your pace, acknowledge your situation, and then decide how you wish to respond to it. In this "pause" you create you can choose a less stressful and more tranquil path.

Self-care allows you to take a break and get away—perhaps through a change of environment or routine, or perhaps only in your mind. This leads to a positive change in perspective. Remind yourself that your current caregiving challenges will change and certainly won't continue forever. If there's a particular problem you need a solution to, self-care will help you with that as well. Your brain works on problems subconsciously without your even knowing it. Once you take a break, you may be surprised to find that a new approach or plan has "appeared," or you accept that the situation can't be changed and will persevere through it in a better frame of mind.

Lowers Levels of Guilt, Anxiety, and Sadness

Self-care can decrease the guilt, anxiety, and sadness that family caregivers often feel. After engaging in self-care, your perspective becomes more balanced with the "positives" in your life, allowing you to face whatever lies ahead that day more easily and with more confidence. Your feelings of frustration will decrease, and you'll experience increased self-worth and peacefulness. You'll be able to acknowledge your strengths and competencies and keep your caregiving concerns in check to a greater degree. Scientists are finding that feeling pleasure can be so stimulating that it primes your brain to respond to pleasure in a way that reinforces it. This means that the more positive experiences you find in your world, the more you will notice around you in return. And, in fact, a landmark study done by Barbara L. Fredrickson, a positive psychology researcher at the University of North Carolina at Chapel Hill, proved that positive emotions help build life satisfaction and reduce symptoms of depression.

CASE STUDY: Benjamin and Self-Care

Benjamin's eighty-five-year-old mother, Rhonda, moved in with him and his wife, Suzie, after she had a stroke and could no longer live on her own. Sharing their home seemed like the perfect solution for their whole family. But as the months passed, Benjamin felt increased levels of anxiety and guilt. After some mindful soul searching, he realized he was spreading himself too thin.

He reached out to Suzie, a registered nurse, for help. Fortunately, she was able to cut back on her work hours and devote time to Rhonda's care. When he made his supervisor aware of his caregiving responsibilities, they came to an arrangement in which Benjamin could leave work early three days a week. The extra time provided immediate relief from his stress and anxiety and became a precious resource Benjamin decided to use for self-care.

With his wife's okay, Benjamin joined a gym and started doing a quick workout before heading home each day. This helped him feel more refreshed mentally, and in time, he noticed he lost some weight and improved muscle tone, which were unexpected bonuses. Benjamin and Suzie took an introductory class on meditation together and incorporated a meditation practice into their morning routine. Waking up thirty minutes earlier to meditate increased the amount of tranquility he had in reserve to call on throughout the day, both at work and while caring for Rhonda. By taking the immediate steps to create some "me time" and then using that time for pleasurable self-care activities, Benjamin became more relaxed and less anxious. His guilt feelings dissipated because he knew he was doing better at taking care of both himself and Rhonda. And Suzie loved their couple's meditation time.

Improves Self-Esteem

Self-care through mindfulness helps improve your self-esteem. When you pause, observe, reflect, and then respond, it puts you in control of the situation, which is an empowering, uplifting feeling. You know you can handle other challenges because you've done it already. As more of these positive outcomes add up, your self-esteem keeps rising. Self-esteem also increases because your self-care actions are feel-good activities of your own choosing. You can't help but have more energy and feel better overall after engaging in something fun or relaxing that you like to do, such as "retail therapy" (shopping in a favorite store), taking a bubble bath, or having a meal with friends.

CONSCIOUS CONNECTIONS

Your friends and loved ones will learn valuable life lessons by observing how you plan time for self-care, and how you honor the commitment made to yourself by following through and taking action. You don't need to talk about your self-care practice or make a big deal about it, but they will notice and remember the behavior model you set for taking care of yourself while caring for another.

It Makes You Happy!

Overall, and in ways that you may not expect, even a little bit of daily self-care goes a long way toward helping you feel like yourself again. After spending between five and twenty minutes doing something enjoyable, you will be less frenzied and feel rejuvenated. Back in a positive frame of mind, you will enjoy your relationships more with dear family and friends. They will be happy to see you smiling more and worrying less too. When viewed through the lens of positive reinforcement, happiness can be seen as an upward spiral—the more joyful activities you do, the more you want to partake in them, and the larger the happiness spiral will grow in diameter.

Happiness feeds upon itself, leading to even more joyful times spent together alone or with friends and family. And, most importantly, when you're in a good place mentally and physically, your care recipient will notice too. You won't even have to tell her you're in a better mood; it will be obvious from how you enter the room that you're in a positive frame of mind. Nonverbal communication—including the smile on your face, your improved posture, and your confident stride—sends a clear message to everyone in your world about how you feel that day.

So now that you know how absolutely important self-care is to your health and happiness and how important it can be for your loved one, it's time to take action and get an idea of how you can fit self-care into your busy life.

HOW TO PRACTICE SELF-CARE

What techniques can you implement to practice self-care? Every human being is different, so your personal self-care plan will be unique. While you find a classical symphony concert relaxing, another person would be bored to tears at one. Part of my self-care plan originated from a favorite childhood activity—taking ballet lessons as a young girl and dreaming of being a ballerina. When I became a family caregiver and needed to find an activity to help me de-stress and decompress, I gravitated back to dance and enrolled in swing dance classes and went social dancing at a local dance studio. Dancing gives me a way to shut off my worries and immerse my mind in learning new steps and techniques. In addition to getting the satisfaction of doing something I love, another benefit of my hobby is knowing it is good for me physically. The social aspects of dancing also gave me an unexpected "bonus": a circle of new and supportive friends. But before we discuss some self-care techniques, let's take a look at what might feel right for you.

EXERCISE: Make a Happiness L.I.S.T.

Self-care can happen while in the midst of caregiving or at a completely separate time and place. It can take numerous forms, based on what makes you feel best. Consider the following questions:

1. What did you love doing as a child? What did you do when you didn't *have* to do anything and were just "hanging out"?
2. What hobbies or interests do you reach for now, as an adult, when you have some free time?
3. Whom do you call first to share great or not-so-great personal news or events with?
4. What environments make you feel good? Which outdoor settings—mountain trails, a peaceful lake, or the beach? Any particular buildings or indoor settings, such as a historic building or library, or do you prefer sitting in front of a crackling fire in a stone fireplace?
5. What sounds and smells make you feel good? Birds chirping? The aroma of bread baking? A crowd cheering for their team at a baseball game? Above all, take the time to reflect on what brings you joy. What relaxes you?

Take a few minutes right now to create a personal, unique Happiness L.I.S.T. (L.I.S.T. stands for Likes, Interests, and Satisfying Things that bring you fulfillment.) Simply jot down five to ten things that make you happy. They can be things that give you joy currently or those you loved previously that you may not indulge in any longer. Think of the activities you do or did when time "disappeared" because you lost track of time while doing them. For example:

- Dancing: Maybe, like me, you loved ballet as a child and have always enjoyed all kinds of dancing.
- Being at the beach: Did you (or do you still) love jumping the waves, playing smash ball in the sand, or collecting seashells?
- Reading: Maybe you love reading books, especially mysteries.
- Playing the guitar: What were (or are) your favorite songs to learn chords to—folk, rock, or country music?
- Planting a vegetable garden: Do you enjoy growing strawberries or tomatoes? Does your garden have room for citrus trees?
- Going to an amusement park: Perhaps you have great memories of going to amusement parks as a child or even as an adult, especially the roller coaster rides.

These passions are yours to continue doing or re-discover again. No matter how far-fetched they may seem, write them all down. This list-making is the beginning of making time for *yourself*, taking action, and not feeling selfish or guilty in doing so. Keep your L.I.S.T. handy to refer to as you continue reading.

Now that you have created your Happiness L.I.S.T., let's look at some popular self-care choices and see if there is some overlap.

Use Meditation

This ancient practice helps train your brain in mindfulness thinking—in how to focus on the moment. It can be a three- to five-minute informal exercise or built up to a longer time period if you like this way of decompressing. Begin by finding a quiet place where you can sit in a tall but comfortable pose. Focus on your natural breathing for a predetermined number of minutes. Using a timer with a gentle-sounding alarm is helpful. Then don't think, which is the hardest part of meditating! When your mind wanders (and it most likely will), notice the thoughts, let them go, and bring your attention back to your breath. Don't critique yourself when this happens; just refocus on your breathing, and continue until the timer goes off. Other alternatives to this traditional form of meditation are standing or walking meditation and doing the Chinese practice of tai chi, which looks like slow-motion dancing.

CONSCIOUS CONNECTIONS

If meditating isn't an option, you can probably manage to take controlled, deep breaths at any time and place. A basic pattern is to both inhale and exhale through your nose to a count of four, pausing and holding in between for another count of four. Continue for as long a time period as you like or until you feel your anxiety level decrease. You may increase to a count of six or eight as you continue this relaxation exercise. Dizziness is not desired, so if you experience any lightheadedness, stop immediately.

Listen to Music

Have you experienced feelings of calm or joy washing over you when you hear a favorite song? If so, you understand the power music has to alter your mood. Soothing music has long been used as a stress management tool because it's a stimulus that evokes memories and emotions. Create playlists of your favorite music to listen to at home, in the car, or while out walking. Music is a matter of personal preference, so choose any songs, no matter the genre, that have significance for you and bring a smile to your face. Thanks to technology, music can be at your fingertips 24/7, so harness that power for relaxation purposes.

CONSCIOUS CONNECTIONS

Make playlists of favorite songs for your care recipient to listen to when she might benefit from a pick-me-up. Classical, patriotic, and big band music have proven popular with the older generation. Also, if you notice that your loved one's home is dimly lit, open the drapes, shutters, shades, and windows to brighten up his immediate surroundings during your visit. Or suggest you go outside together and visit a nearby park or take a scenic drive.

Vent

Sometimes you need to have a good cry, so allow it to happen. I'd be upbeat and all smiles while visiting my mom, but as soon as I'd close her front door behind me and head for home, the tears would flow. It's 100 percent okay to cry because family caregiving is not easy! Another way to vent is by writing a letter to yourself or your loved one, pouring out all of your emotions onto paper. But *don't mail it* because it is intended for your eyes only. Shred it after a while instead. A third way to vent is to drive to an isolated (but safe) location, make sure the car windows are up, and scream. Release your feelings of frustration and anger there, rather than letting them build up until you "explode," yelling at your care recipient or other family members because you're at the end of your rope.

Use Your Happiness L.I.S.T.

Pull out the list you made earlier of five to ten things that bring you happiness. Look them over and select one thing that will make you feel like you're spoiling yourself. Now think of a way you can incorporate this action into your day, even if in an abbreviated or slightly altered way.

It may be easier to put yourself first if you start with only one or two of the items you wrote down on your list. Begin by doing things that take a short amount of time, and then you will likely increase the time you spend doing them, because you will see the positive effects self-care has in your life. For example, maybe as a child you took ballet, and dancing always brought you joy. Do you have a family member or friend who you can go out dancing with one evening for a few hours? Or does your local parks and recreation department offer group dance classes? If so, try one! Even just one class a week for one month will be helpful. Losing yourself in the movement and music will help clear your head of the caregiving worries you live with constantly.

Maybe your list includes your love of the beach? If you live near one now, it's well worth the time away from caregiving to take a walk on the beach every once in a while. It will rejuvenate you and make you ready to face caregiving realities once again. It's sometimes hard to do, but leaving your normal physical surroundings causes a shift in perspective and attitude. So get out of your routine however possible and do something that makes you feel fulfilled.

Use Time Effectively

Everyone has the same twenty-four hours in a day to get things done, minus sleep, of course. But caregivers have more things on their lists than the average person does. Using your time effectively will help your day go more smoothly, you'll get the most important things done, and you'll feel a sense of fulfillment through your accomplishments by day's end. (Plus, you'll find more time to engage in a fun activity on your Happiness L.I.S.T.!)

EXERCISE: Create a Master To-Do List

Start to implement time management skills by making a master to-do list of everything you want to get done, both short and long term. This master list can include separate categories for caregiving, family, work, volunteering, and personal areas in your life. Then prioritize the master list from the most important to least important items, and also guesstimate how long these items may take. If you've set up categories within the master list, prioritize each of those categories separately. Priorities can be assigned based on importance and urgency. Then take the top priorities from these longer lists and put them on a new, daily to-do list. You may need to take a large task and break it into smaller pieces in time periods over a few days. For example, if your father needs help cleaning out his garage before selling his house, plan on doing that task together for a few hours each Saturday over the next three weekends.

Here's an example of how your master list should look, with priorities marked in parentheses. This sample list combines Family and Personal areas into one category. You can break out the areas however you like best. From this master list select the highest-priority items from each area to put on your daily to-do list.

Try not to let your daily to-do list overwhelm you. Realize and accept that you may not get everything done on your list that day and that's perfectly okay. Select three of the most important things to accomplish and focus on those first. When you get those done, take time out to congratulate yourself! This is a good time to take a break and choose something from your Happiness L.I.S.T. as a reward. Caregivers are so busy helping others, they tend to not acknowledge and congratulate themselves when they reach their goals. Be proud of everything you accomplish during the day, every day, no matter how big or small these accomplishments are. Many people don't give themselves credit, especially for the smaller victories. Be aware of this and pat yourself on the back for every task you complete or goal you reach. After taking a break, continue on with the next priorities on your list.

MASTER TO-DO LIST

Caregiving for Mom	*Work*	*Family and Personal*	*Volunteering*
(2) Make an appointment with neurologist (Dr. Stevens, 123-456-XXXX).	(4) Set up meeting with committee about annual industry convention—will we have booth and what will the theme be?	(2) Buy 8th birthday card and gift for nephew Joe (party on Sunday at 2 p.m., Erica's house).	(2) Call church coordinator to get office volunteer schedule for next month. Discuss any time conflicts and rearrange my hours if necessary.
(1) Fill and pick up new Rx (CVS, 123-456-XXXX).	(1) Complete XYZ project due by end of this week.	(4) Check that my dress, shoes, and purse are ready for Smith wedding at end of month. Purchase gift and card from bride's gift registry (Bed Bath & Beyond or Macy's).	(1) Decide on and order floral centerpieces for business networking lunch event next week.
(3) Buy 3 cartons of Depends adult diapers (ladies size S) at Costco.	(3) Check my vacation time and request days off.	(3) Schedule haircut and style.	(3) Call gala committee chairperson re: my assignment for next year's gala, and would like to be teamed up again with Diane.

Caregiving for Mom	Work	Family and Personal	Volunteering
(5) Send family and friends email with her new address after her move to Oasis Senior Living.	(2) Schedule annual performance review with my three assistants before HR deadline in two weeks.	(1) Schedule dentist about pain that comes and goes in lower left molar (Dr. King, 123-456-XXXX).	
(4) Take her for haircut. Find closest hair salon to new home.	(5) Look into company's new vanpooling options.	(5) Connect with cousins about our annual Cousins Weekend this year.	

Realize that keeping your priorities intact may mean you have to say no to other people's requests. Caregivers by nature usually want to help everyone, but you're learning how to put yourself first now. Instead of saying yes and feeling resentful, practice saying the following sentence when you're asked to do something you don't have time or energy for:

> "I really would like to help you, but I'm not in a position to do that right now."

At the end of each day, revisit your daily and master lists and write a new to-do list for the next day. It's helpful to do this the night before to feel organized when you awaken and not have to figure out where to begin again each morning.

And most importantly, don't berate yourself if you don't get everything done on your daily list! Unexpected things happen, especially during the caregiving years, and it won't be the end of the world if you carry over tasks to the next day.

Stay Healthy

Taking care of your physical health is an important part of self-care and increased longevity, and it's an area that many people overlook. You need to try your best to stay in top shape physically so you're not distracted by nagging symptoms of ailments and can maintain the physical strength and stamina needed to care for your loved one.

If you've ever experienced feelings of "doom and gloom" when you're under the weather, you know how important good health is for a family caregiver's perspective and attitude too. When not at the top of your game physically, the resulting crankiness and negative outlook that you exhibit can spill over into everything (and everyone) around you. That's the last thing you and your loved one need.

Here are some ways to stay in tip-top shape:

Eat Healthy

People are often so busy that they don't eat regularly or they grab fast food instead of nutritious choices for meals. But even if you're pressed for time you can still opt for healthy meal choices. How?

- Even if you don't have time to prepare three meals a day, most grocery stores and restaurants offer nutritious take-out menu items that will keep you on track. Get in the habit of reading food labels to learn serving size and nutrition information. Aim for a balanced diet of whole grains, fruits and vegetables, protein, and dairy, while keeping fat and sugar to a minimum.
- Alleviate the worry about what you and your family will have for dinner each night. Spend time one weeknight (or over the weekend if you work full-time) planning, shopping for, and preparing meals in advance. Use plastic containers to

refrigerate or freeze individual dishes you and your family can grab as needed.

- Keep a supply of healthy snack foods handy, such as fruit, yogurt, and granola bars. Snacking throughout the day keeps your hunger under control and will help keep you from overeating later in the day.
- Make wholesome food choices when grocery shopping. Avoid buying foods with lots of sugar, preservatives, and empty calories. (Although as part of self-care I treat myself every day to chocolate, even if it's eating just one piece of candy or one chocolate chip cookie. And yes, it's possible to eat just one!)
- Don't skip breakfast. Dietitians still agree it is the most important meal of the day because it provides your body with necessary energy and is an important source of essential nutrients, protein, and fiber. Research has shown that if these are missed at breakfast, they are less likely to be made up for later in the day. Eating a healthy breakfast also helps concentration and productivity all day.
- Remember to stay hydrated by drinking lots of water throughout the day. A popular way to measure is the "8 by 8" rule: drink eight 8-ounce glasses of water or fluids per day. All fluids count toward your daily total, but water should be the majority of this measure.

If you start eating in a more healthy way now, this new habit will hopefully continue throughout the rest of your life, long after your caregiving journey is over.

Get Some Sleep

According to the Mayo Clinic, adults need seven to nine hours of sleep per night—and the quality of your sleep is just as important as quantity. Research done at Harvard Medical School's Division of Sleep

Medicine, including a study by Dr. Janet Mullington, has shown that insufficient sleep on a regular basis can lead to health issues, such as obesity, type 2 diabetes, high blood pressure, and heart disease. Chronic sleep issues may also correlate to depression, anxiety, and stress and are associated with lower life expectancy.

As a caregiver, you may have trouble getting a good night's sleep consistently due to the many concerns and worries you have on your mind. However, there are habits you can develop that will decrease insomnia and improve your sleep, including:

- Avoid caffeine, alcohol, and nicotine for four to six hours before bedtime. Try drinking some chamomile tea thirty minutes before bed. According to researchers, chamomile is associated with an increase of glycine, a chemical that acts like a mild sedative and relaxes your nerves and muscles. Caffeine and nicotine are both stimulants that make it harder to fall asleep and stay asleep. According to the Sleep Health Foundation, although alcohol may make you feel sleepy and help you fall asleep initially, it actually disrupts your sleep in the second half of the night through more frequent awakenings, night sweats, and nightmares.
- Create an environment built around the basic conditions needed for a good night's sleep. Make your bedroom a sleep-inducing space by keeping it cool, well ventilated, and dark. It's essential to have warm hands and feet, but being too hot overall is not conducive to good sleep. Turn off the TV and try using a white-noise machine or earplugs to block outside sounds because it's harder to fall asleep if the room is even slightly noisy. When was the last time you bought a new mattress and pillows? People often don't realize the age of their bed's important components. Make sure you are comfortable from head to toe when lying down.

- Avoid doing stressful, stimulating activities an hour or so before bed. Don't work from bed. Your mind needs to get in the habit of knowing that if you're in bed, you are there to sleep. Staying away from the light of digital screens for a few hours has been proven helpful for inducing sleep. The blue light emitted by screens on cell phones, computers, tablets, and TVs inhibits the production of melatonin, the hormone that controls your sleep-wake cycle. Try keeping your bedtime and the time you wake up consistent, even on weekends, in order to set your body's internal clock.
- If you can't fall asleep, don't toss and turn for more than twenty minutes. Sleep experts agree that trying to make yourself fall asleep is counterproductive at that point. Get up, go into another room, but keep the lights dim. Do something relaxing for a little while, such as listening to mellow music. Choose something calm and soothing versus an activity that will rev you up. When you feel a wave of tiredness come over you, then head back to bed. Repeat this same pattern if you awaken during the night and can't get back to sleep.
- If you find your sleep has been interrupted, try taking a "power nap" (twenty minutes maximum) during the next day to rejuvenate yourself.

A good night's sleep is important to everyone's health and well-being, and especially for caregivers.

Get Active

Studies show that exercising regularly leads to improved physical fitness, higher self-esteem, decreases in anxiety and depression, and improved sleep—all things a family caregiver will benefit from. Try to exercise for twenty to thirty minutes at a time, ideally three days a week. But, again, don't stress about trying to get exercise into your busy schedule. Some days it might not happen, and that's okay. Pick the types of exercise you enjoy doing so you look forward to it.

The Centers for Disease Control and Prevention (CDC) recommend that adults do two types of physical activity each week: aerobic and muscle-strengthening.

- Aerobic or "cardio" exercises are any activities that get you breathing harder and your heart beating faster. These can include brisk walking, jogging, swimming, tennis, bike riding, and even pushing a lawn mower. One way to tell that you're working at a moderate-intensity aerobic level is that you'll be able to speak, but not sing, the words to your favorite song. At a vigorous-intensity level of exercise you won't be able to say more than a few words without pausing for a breath.
- Muscle-strengthening exercises should work out the major muscle groups of your body (legs, hips, back, chest, shoulders, abdomen, and arms). These can be done at home or at a gym and might include activities such as lifting weights, using resistance bands, heavy gardening, or yoga.

You can also give dance a try! Along with the physical fitness and weight loss benefits, dancing improves your mood. Science has proven that dancing reduces stress hormones and stimulates the production of endorphins, the chemicals responsible for triggering positive feelings. The style of dance you do is entirely up to you. Dancing can range from taking progressive, weekly group classes or private lessons at a local dance studio to spontaneously dancing freestyle around your own house in total privacy. Moving to music in any way helps clear your head by taking the focus away from your worries and pointing your thoughts toward physical actions.

Stay on Top of *Your* Medical Issues

Another aspect of self-care is being tuned in to your own body and seeing a doctor when needed. Many caregivers are wonderful about taking their care recipients to their doctors' appointments, yet many don't make the time for their own regular checkups. If this sounds like you, don't neglect your own routine doctor visits. And if you notice aches, pains, lumps, bruises, or anything unusual for your own body, see your doctor within a few days or weeks, not months later. Medical problems that might easily be taken care of can become more complicated if you delay. Don't put it off, because if something happens to you, then what will your care recipient do?

Pamper Yourself

Choosing to do more of what nourishes you rather than depletes you is a way to practice self-care as a conscious caregiver. When was the last time you had a massage? A manicure or pedicure? Took a walk in a favorite place? Had a "date night" with your spouse? Shared a meal with a dear friend? Some of these ideas might already be on your Happiness L.I.S.T., but if not, even brief sojourns of your choice are ways to indulge yourself. Put these dates on the calendar, and keep them. Your care recipient will wait the extra time that these activities take. And you will return to your caregiving responsibilities with a more relaxed and positive perspective, ready to take on whatever the next day brings.

Add a Dose of Laughter

The adage "Laughter is the best medicine" is correct. Simply put, laughing makes us feel better. A few ways to inject humor into your day are: Listening to comedy or positive-thinking podcasts or radio shows. Watching favorite comics' routines on *YouTube* or funny TV shows. (This partly explains why reruns of the classic *I Love Lucy* episodes are still popular to this day.) Telling jokes to and with your friends or family. Watching dog and cat videos on *YouTube*. Reading humorous or joke books. Observing the world around you for funny situations that happen right under your nose. (Not laughing *at* people, laughing *with* them.) As a family caregiver in a tough situation, think about how you can find a way to choose laughter over tears.

CASE STUDY: Denise and Laughter

Denise's husband, Eric, was suffering from Lou Gehrig's disease (ALS) and could no longer shave. As disheartening as this was for both of them, Denise describes her lighthearted approach: "Eric was quite a kidder. I'd say 'Do you think I can do this today without actually making you bleed somewhere? You know this is not a leg and that's what I'm used to shaving. Is there any trick you can show me?' And we'd just make a joke out of it and laugh together."

By approaching the situation in this lighthearted way and focusing on her inability to shave rather than his, Denise was able to mitigate the sadness they both felt about his declining health. Her teasing and joking around was part of the self-care she chose in order to keep her attitude upbeat.

"A good laugh and a long sleep are the two best cures for anything."

—Irish proverb

CHAPTER SUMMARY

The following are takeaways, action steps, and reminders to help your caregiving journey progress smoothly.

- As a family caregiver you must go against your instincts and put yourself first. If you ignore your own needs, this could lead to an unhealthy level of caregiver stress and/or burnout. After you begin practicing self-care this "you time" will grow into a habit you look forward to every day.
- The positive benefits of self-care practices include improved physical and mental health, lower stress levels, and improved levels of happiness.
- Create a Happiness L.I.S.T. (Likes, Interests, and Satisfying Things) of personal pleasures that are either current passions or things you loved in childhood that you stopped doing. Include activities that cause you to lose all sense of time. You'll be surprised at the creative ways you can fit your passions into your day. Continue to refer to and use your Happiness L.I.S.T. throughout your caregiving journey.
- Conscious caregiving and self-care begin by practicing mindfulness, or self-awareness in the present moment without judging yourself and others. You stop whatever actions you're engaged in, pause, and pay attention, taking in your immediate surroundings through your senses. You don't criticize, praise, or label what you observe. Then carefully decide if there are thoughts or actions you can change in order to create an improved situation for you and/or your loved one.
- Time management will make your days go more smoothly and help you discover time for self-care. Make a master to-do list, and then break it down into sub-lists, such as caregiving, family, work, volunteer, and personal. Then prioritize the most important one with three things you feel you can accomplish comfortably in one

day. Reward yourself with a treat for everything you *do* accomplish each day! Don't beat yourself up if you don't get to them all. Just put them on the next day's list and continue on.

- Maintaining your physical health can be accomplished by eating nutritious meals, getting adequate sleep, and including some form of exercise every day. Don't put off seeing your doctors for regular checkups, if you notice any new ailments, or if you experience increased levels of stress or anxiety. What will your loved one do if something happens to you and you can't care for her?
- Pamper yourself. Choose things to do that nourish your body, mind, or spirit. What activity or activities have you done from your Happiness L.I.S.T. today? Get started now!

PART 2

The Art of Conscious Communication

CHAPTER 4

Conscious Communication with Your Loved One

Throughout your life your family relationships have likely been grounded in interpersonal communication. As a baby and youngster you learned your first communication skills at home and then took those skills out into the world with you. You continued to learn more skills and refine your communication style by applying them in a variety of situations in your schooling, relationships, and career. Due to many years of shared experiences family members often develop their own "shorthand" and ingrained habits when speaking with each other. You often read each other's minds with just a glance at the other's face or body language. But when caregiving begins, that comfortable family "lingo" can cause problems and lead to hurt.

Prior family dynamics, such as childhood sibling rivalry, can reappear when adult children start caring for their aging parents. Prior bad feelings or conflicts you haven't given thought to for years, or believed were resolved long ago, may resurface and be expressed through words of jealousy or competitiveness. Since you are all adults with new roles, your past roles and ingrained speaking patterns need to change. As a caregiver, you need to become acutely aware of the words you're using and how they sound to your loved one as well as other family team members. Communicating clearly and kindly makes caregiving easier and more successful.

In this chapter, ways to be more mindful in all aspects of communication are provided, along with specific tips on how to communicate with the hearing-impaired and those with memory loss. Here you'll also find strategies for starting hard conversations with the people closest to you. Read on to learn how to communicate as part of conscious caregiving.

MINDFUL COMMUNICATION IS THE GOAL

Clear and open communication is made up of three parts:

1. Listening
2. Speaking
3. Nonverbal communication

It's important to practice these skills to the best of your ability while you're a family caregiver. And they need to be done thoughtfully, with mindfulness at the core of the exchange. Remember to pause, observe, reflect, and then speak.

Mindful Listening

In your desire to "get things done" for your loved one, you may feel so rushed during a visit that you don't take time to have a meaningful conversation. Your care recipient may be declining physically, but as long as his or her cognitive abilities are fine, she has the right to state preferences and drive the decisions that need to be made. It may take more time than you allotted and complicate your day, but take time to listen patiently and afford your loved one the respect she has earned.

Allow her to share not only wishes but also fears, concerns, and feelings about this final stage of life.

Through mindful listening—the act of focusing completely on what others say as well as how they express themselves—you let your loved one know that you are partnering with her, and not taking over her life. People generally listen with only "half an ear"—they immediately start thinking about and formulating their response, rather than completely hearing the message the other person is expressing. Other poor listening habits people often exhibit are interrupting their loved ones and finishing their sentences for them. So take the time to slow down the conversation. Pause, really focus, and listen attentively and comprehensively in that very moment. Then think about your loved one's words, including the underlying feelings those words represent, *before* you think about your reply. Only after completing those steps should you speak.

EXERCISE: Record Your Conversations

Listening for the umpteenth time as your father explains how he and his brothers started their business together may drive you crazy, but these family stories are precious. Just because you can recite them word for word along with your loved one right now doesn't mean you will always recall every detail. Record these conversations with your loved one, either via audio or video. Years later, after he has passed away, you'll be glad you took the time to preserve these bits of family history. Or, if your parent or relative is still able, have her write the stories in a journal as a way of giving her life purpose and deeper meaning. It doesn't have to be a complete, formal autobiography; instead urge your loved one to write down favorite anecdotes in whatever order she thinks of them, or write whatever she feels like writing about on that particular day. Anything recorded for future generations is better than nothing.

Mindful Speaking

The words you speak can have subtle yet powerful effects on those around you. Words said aloud, and even what you say to yourself in your own head, make a difference in how you think and feel about others, yourself, and your actions. Behaviors are influenced by thoughts, and words are often a direct reflection of these thoughts. Bringing compassion into your caregiving language by speaking mindfully will reap positive results. Thinking before you speak is a mindfulness skill that allows you to select more compassionate words in your conversations and helps prevent misunderstandings. First, truly listen to your conversation partner. Then take time to process what he has said before responding with the first thing that jumps into your head or with worn-out phrases you use repeatedly with your loved one, such as "Everything will be all right." Pause. Listen. Think. Then respond in the kindest way possible.

For example, would you describe an aging loved one who is losing some ability to function as "deteriorating" or "declining"? There is only a small distinction between these descriptors, yet your choice clearly creates very different thoughts and feelings for whomever is listening. The word *deteriorating* has a harsher and more negative connotation than what the word *declining* conjures up. When something or someone deteriorates, it's often from lack of attention or care, and that is certainly not the case with your loved one. If a person were describing you or someone you love, which of those two terms would you prefer? Which is the more compassionate word to choose? The same is true for using *care recipient* rather than *patient. Patient* usually refers to someone ill or in need of health care. Not all care recipients are in poor health. Some may just need assistance with the "heavy-lifting" chores at home, such as laundry, yard work, or grocery shopping. The term *care recipient* is a more inclusive description of someone in need of any type of assistance provided by a caregiver, no matter what his health status may be.

Another critical time to use mindful speaking is when you're planning to address difficult topics with your loved one, which we will address in depth later in this chapter. It's helpful to consider your goals, motivations, and perspectives before engaging in conversation about a particular issue.

Mindful Nonverbal Communication

Nonverbal communication is defined as communicating without speech. It can include facial expressions, eye contact, touch, tone of voice, posture, gestures, and proximity between people. Powerful messages can be sent in various ways without speaking a word. Nonverbal signals can add meaning above and beyond the words being said.

Body Language

Become aware of the nonverbal signals you are transmitting to your loved one. Do you roll your eyes or shake your head from side to side (as in "no") while she is talking? Do you stand with your hands clenched or arms crossed in front of your chest? How far away are you sitting while conversing? These could all be sending negative vibes in spite of what your spoken words convey.

Become conscious and mindful of your facial and bodily movements and positioning and consider how your nonverbal cues are affecting your loved one. Send positive nonverbal messages that reinforce your care and concern. Sit or stand in a relaxed posture. Be close enough to gently touch your loved one's arm or back, keep eye contact, and don't frown when you're listening to her point of view.

Tone of Voice

Your tone of voice is also crucial. Be aware of the volume and pitch of your voice during conversations with your loved one. Are you using your normal speaking voice? If you hear yourself speaking at a louder volume than usual, is it because you're talking over background noise or because you're upset with your loved one?

Be sure to speak to your care recipient the same way you wish to be spoken to—with respect. Try your hardest not to speak harshly, no matter how stressed you're feeling in the moment. If you feel you want to yell at your loved one, walk away—either into another room or outside—until you are calm again.

Your Loved One's Nonverbal Communication

Nonverbal communication is a two-way street, and it's equally important to notice what your loved one's gestures and body language reflect as it is your own. Observe his posture, face, and voice. What does this input tell you about how he is feeling right now? Might he be responding to your words, behavior, and degree of calm or upset? Does your loved one break eye contact with you repeatedly during a conversation? That might be a cue that he doesn't want to continue the discussion. He could be tired, distracted, or simply not ready to speak about the topic. Be sensitive to and show respect for the nonverbal signals your care recipient subconsciously sends. During conversation, if you affectionately touch your loved one's arm and he moves away, this is a clear message that he doesn't want to be touched at that time. Accept this nonverbal behavioral response and don't take it personally.

> "The single biggest problem in communication is the illusion that it has taken place."
>
> —William H. Whyte, American urbanist

ADDRESSING DIFFICULT ISSUES

There will be times when you'll need to speak with your aging parents about topics that are uncomfortable and/or difficult to discuss, such as allowing you or another family member to manage their finances, moving from their home into assisted living, no longer driving, hiring in-home caregivers, and making decisions about end-of-life care, funerals, and estate plans.

In order for these conversations to go more smoothly, it helps to take a mindful approach in your communications. This can be done while you're engaged in a particular interaction or used in a broader context, such as in the planning stages before conversing about a bigger problem or issue. Remember the mindfulness steps: pause, observe, reflect, and then take action, or in this case, speak. As a conscious caregiver, first think carefully on your own about the issue you want to address before you broach the subject with your care recipient. This includes doing research if needed and giving the topic careful consideration for a period of days or weeks, not just in the hour prior to seeing your loved one. These difficult issues are complex, can affect several family members, and are best thought through from multiple perspectives, including the following:

Consider Your Emotional Response

Consider why the topic is difficult for you to talk about. Examine your own fears or insecurities on the subject. For example, most people in our society don't want to even think about death, let alone speak about it with their loved ones. Recognize and come to terms with your own thoughts and feelings before delving into a conversation. Otherwise your own emotional response may catch you off guard and hinder the conversation's progress.

EXERCISE:
Come to Terms with Your Emotions

On a piece of paper, write a brief description of the issue you want to address with your loved one(s). Create three columns below it, covering the emotions you feel, why you think you have those feelings, and how you can best deal with those emotions before speaking with your care recipient.

TOPIC: My parents need to move out of their home of forty years into an assisted living community.		
How Do You Feel?	*Why Are You Feeling That Way?*	*How Will You Deal with That Emotion?*
Nervous	Not sure how they will react to the idea of moving because we haven't talked about it before.	Knowledge calms my nerves. Read books about caring for aging parents and moving into assisted living. Ask other friends who have gone through this how it went.
Sad	Because having to move reflects in no uncertain terms that they are both aging and declining. They are bound to feel sadness, too, so I'm sharing in their pain.	Remember to focus on the fact that their safety is the #1 priority and this is why they have to move. It's no longer safe for them to live on their own in the house. Moving to assisted living is the best solution under the circumstances.
Resentful	Because my sister is choosing not to be involved in this big change, due to her own personal circumstances, whether real or imagined.	Have one more conversation to try to enlist her help. Don't get angry, but let her know I feel disappointed and why/how I need her assistance. If she still refuses to help, then proceed as if I were an only child, knowing I can do this competently on my own.
Sentimental	This is my childhood home with many fond memories that I will no longer be able to visit after it's sold.	Recognize and accept that this is a normal rite of passage many people go through. Allow plenty of time to sort through childhood keepsakes there. Decide to either move these items to my home, or take digital photos as a way to hold onto them forever.

Writing down your feelings, thinking them through, and coming to terms with them helps you mentally prepare for the conversations ahead. As a conscious caregiver with a peaceful heart and mind, you will be better able to focus on your loved one's responses and input.

Let Your Loved One Participate

Clarify this fact in your own mind: are you having this conversation *with* your care recipient or *for* her? If you're going to be discussing a safety issue, she may not have veto power over the decision you see as necessary. This will affect how you present the issue and its possible solutions. For example, your mother has "misplaced" her credit card three times in the past nine months. Rather than brainstorming yet another solution to fix this recurring problem, at this point you want to present only one option: to protect her from fraud and possible identity theft she must surrender her credit card. After telling her your decision and why, you can then discuss other ways she can pay for things instead of using her credit card. But if her cognitive abilities are intact and safety isn't an issue, her active participation, goals, and wishes should remain in the forefront of the decision-making process.

CASE STUDY: Peggy and Difficult Conversations

Peggy, a caregiving daughter, shares how she came to manage her parents' finances as their health declined:

She says, "For me, one of the hardest parts of helping my parents as they aged was trying to find the balance between being respectful of their wishes and desires for their lives, and what I thought was the right thing for them to do. That was a very difficult balance to strike, and I don't know that I ever really found the right balance. You can only do the best you can do.

"It was very frustrating for my parents to have to ask me for help. They didn't like being in that situation, especially my father. It was funny because, in the beginning, if we'd talk about finances, he would say, 'Your husband has to be here.' He would not accept that I could do it. Then, at one point after he had been hospitalized, he realized that my mother was in no way going to be able to stay on top of everything, so at that point he willingly gave me control of his finances, but I don't think he ever liked it. I always said it was like I was an invisible chauffeur driving from the trunk of his car. My actions were out of sight, yet I was the one moving things along for them. I wanted to maintain his dignity by letting him remain in the 'driver's seat' so to speak. It was *his* life he had created and *his* finances. He had every right to make those decisions, because cognitively I knew he was quite able to and *deserved* to. It was his place to make the decisions, but then I was the one who had to implement them, so it was a very difficult balancing act."

Set Realistic Goals

Set a realistic goal for the conversation, and tackle small parts of a large change in a series of conversations over time. This gives your loved one time to absorb the new ideas and give thoughtful consideration to these modifications too. Don't assume your loved one will agree to a major life change in one sitting. For example, do you really need to see your parents' complete financial portfolio, or are you trying to find out something specific, such as if they have placed their assets in a family trust? Be transparent and make certain that your requests reflect only your exact needs. Ask if you can see their trust documents in order to answer a particular question their estate attorney had. Being open and honest will build their trust in you and your ability to handle their care overall. Remember, while you've taken time to think over changes you'd like to see, your initial conversation is the first they've heard about it, so give them plenty of time to process your suggestions. Focusing on the specifics of what you want to address in each conversation will go a long way toward ensuring a smooth discussion and will help you avoid conflict.

CONSCIOUS CONNECTIONS

According to *Caregiving in the U.S. 2015*, 22 percent of caregivers self-reported their health had gotten worse as a result of caregiving, and this toll increased over time. Caring for a close relative, such as a spouse or parent (45 percent and 44 percent, respectively), is more emotionally stressful for caregivers than caring for another relative (35 percent) or non-relative (18 percent).

Do Your Research

Do your homework before sitting down to have a difficult discussion with your loved one. Research the topic first, and bring notes with information you want to share. You want to have as many facts as possible at your fingertips and be prepared to answer his or her questions. Make two copies of the relevant information, and leave one with your care recipient to review. Writing down your ideas before you get together with your loved one provides you with time to express yourself clearly when you're centered and focused and anticipate possible questions. Plus, the act of writing down your thoughts helps eliminate the "it sounded good in my head" phenomenon and lets your brain "practice" what you wish to express. It also helps to read what you want to say out loud to yourself to make sure the chosen words are appropriate for the upcoming conversation. This way, you will have the kindest words ready to use, rather than replying quickly (and quite possibly emotionally) on the spot.

Remember, the words you choose to speak matter even more when the topics are difficult. For example, don't say you want to talk with your loved one about "taking the car keys away," because that emphasizes a loss of power and independence. Rather, phrase the discussion this way: "Can we please talk about cutting back on how much you drive?" You can follow up in a later conversation with, "Here are some transportation alternatives I thought you might like to read and think about. Perhaps we can try them out together during my next few visits."

Keep Time in Mind

Carefully select the best time to start a deep conversation. If you know your aging parents are more energetic in the morning, you may want to see them then rather than later in the afternoon when they are more likely to be tired or need a nap. Catching seniors at their optimal time of day can help discussions go more smoothly because they will be at their sharpest for communicating.

As family caregiver, you, too, should be well rested and calm when you know you will be tackling a hard subject. Don't start a lengthy discussion when any of you are feeling stressed or tired, mentally or physically.

Allow ample time for the conversations and ultimately for any decisions to unfold. Don't rush the conversation to a conclusion, because that may prove frustrating for you or your care recipient. As people age, it takes longer to do things, which includes processing questions and new ideas. This is especially true if it's the first time you're broaching a hard subject. Many of these potentially emotional topics will need to be discussed several times before decisions are reached. Realize this from the start, and don't push for hasty decisions.

Choose an Appropriate Location

Carefully consider where to meet. Select a place free of distractions and interruptions—not a restaurant or outdoors. If you think your loved ones will be happiest talking about private matters in their own home, meet there. Before you begin, make sure the TV and everyone's cell phones are turned off and none of you needs to head off soon to another activity or appointment. Think about the seating arrangements, too, especially if the conversation may go long. Is everyone seated in comfortable chairs and able to see and hear each other well? All of these factors contribute to a more relaxed and focused conversation.

Don't Avoid Difficult Conversations

Do not avoid conversations if they involve the safety of your loved one or other people around her. It's natural to want to put off these difficult conversations, but that won't make the decisions any easier. Waiting will only increase the potential risk to your loved one and others. And it is always better to make decisions beforehand, rather than when you're in the midst of a crisis.

For example, if your mother falls and breaks her shoulder, it will be hard to be with her in the hospital and also be touring care facilities where she will have to move. If you and your mom have already decided upon your top one or two local eldercare facilities beforehand, it will keep both of your stress levels lower and allow you to have a shorter and simpler conversation than if you had to start from scratch when she's not feeling great. And since she was part of the process and decision previously, she won't feel like you're telling her what to do.

Nearly every caregiver interviewed for this book admitted that having their loved one stop driving was one of the hardest challenges they faced. Giving up driving entails a loss of independence visible to the world, plus an admission that the person's physical and/or thinking capabilities are weaker. No longer driving also triggers a big lifestyle change for your loved one and could affect other family members who must then become their chauffeurs. However, opening up this conversation with your loved one before driving becomes dangerous is incredibly important for your loved one's safety and the safety of those around her.

CASE STUDY: Denise and the Dreaded Driving Issue

Denise, age sixty-two, is the caregiving daughter for her mother, Lorraine, age eighty-eight. One day Lorraine mentioned that she was having trouble getting the car into "park." After a test-drive, Denise expressed her worries: "Here's my concern, Mom. If you cannot get the car in 'park' and your foot pushes down on the gas pedal, you could go through your garage wall into the backyard. Or, if you're in a parking lot and there are people walking behind you or in front of you and that happens, you would hit them. You'll change their lives and ours forever, and I can't imagine living with something like that if there are choices you can make to prevent it."

Denise also raised the point that Lorraine would probably be happier if *she* made the decision to stop driving herself, rather than if the doctor, the DMV, or Denise made the decision for her. Lorraine agreed to think about it and, a few days later, agreed to stop driving. However, a few days after that, Denise found her mother's car moved out of its parking spot in the driveway, and Lorraine admitted to moving it. Denise then told her mom that at the end of their visit, she'd be taking all of the car keys with her that day, and *any* driving to be done from then on would be done only by Denise. Luckily, Lorraine agreed. Denise feels fortunate that they didn't have arguments, even if it took a while to get the details worked out. And while Denise definitely encouraged it, Lorraine still feels she made the decision herself.

COMMUNICATING WITH THE HEARING-IMPAIRED

While hearing loss affects all age groups, aging is a common cause of hearing loss. In age-related hearing loss (presbycusis), changes in the inner ear cause slow but steady hearing loss. These changes can range from mild to severe, but they are always permanent. Communicating with hearing-impaired older adults can be very challenging, and you may find yourself becoming frustrated or angry. Perhaps your care recipient would benefit from the use of a hearing aid, yet he refuses to wear one or is struggling with hearing loss in some other way. In this case, you want to communicate with him with kindness, patience, information sharing, and a series of conversations over time. Here are some tips to help you do this:

Considerations Before You Speak

How you approach someone with hearing loss and the environment you are in make a difference. Here are some things to think about in order to set the stage:

- Be sure your loved one sees you approaching so you don't startle her. If you realize she doesn't see you approaching, gently touch her on the arm or shoulder to announce your presence before you begin speaking.
- Once you have your loved one's attention, stand or sit directly in front of him with your faces at the same level. Don't speak to him from behind or from the side. Positioning yourself three to six feet away is optimal for listening or lip reading.
- Check the lighting to be sure you aren't backlit so your loved one isn't looking at a dark silhouette against a bright background. Try to have lighting on your face. Check that the sun or a bright light isn't shining directly into her eyes.
- Reduce or eliminate background noise, such as music, TVs, fans, and other conversations around you. While this isn't always possible, there are helpful choices you can make. For example, eat in your loved one's home rather than going out to a dimly lit and noisy restaurant where conversation may prove difficult or nearly impossible.
- If you go to a restaurant or other event with your loved one, strategic seating may improve his ability to hear. When possible have him sit against a wall, because in that position sounds will be coming from only 180 degrees rather than 360 degrees. If the wall has textured wall covering, that can help muffle sounds further.

Paying attention to these details before speaking will improve the quality of your conversation.

Face-to-Face Conversations

The use of these communication strategies will lead to more successful exchanges with those who have hearing loss.

- Speak slowly and clearly in a normal tone of voice. Do not shout. When you raise your voice, the sound becomes distorted and incomprehensible. Those who wear hearing aids might even find listening to shouting to be painful due to the amplification of sounds.
- Do not exaggerate your lip movements. That makes it more difficult for someone who is lip reading to understand the words you are speaking.
- Use simple, short sentences to make comprehension easier. Trying to follow longer, complex sentences is harder for hearing-impaired people. The same difficulty arises if someone speaks rapidly and/or doesn't pause between sentences.
- It helps not to chew gum or eat while talking. People with hearing loss listen actively as you form your words, and that often includes lip reading. Chewing distorts the lip movements, making it difficult to connect the movements to the sounds. Also, do your best to keep your hands away from your face. If the person clearly sees your lips, she can usually connect the sounds with your lip movements, even if she is not trained formally in lip reading.
- If your loved one doesn't understand what you're saying, try rephrasing it using different but still simple words.
- Utilize nonverbal means of communication to supplement your words. Provide visual cues though your facial expressions and natural gestures, such as giving a thumbs-up or thumbs-down.
- Try not to jump from subject to subject. Let your loved one know you are changing the topic and allow him time to focus on the new discussion.

If all else fails, write down your words in a spiral notebook or binder for your loved one to read. Be sure your handwriting is legible. Allow time for her to read your question, think it over, and then give an answer verbally. An added benefit of writing is that your care recipient then has a record of your visits and can "replay" them by reading through the notebook. When using this technique, be sure the lighting in the room is adequate for reading.

You can also make a notebook with laminated pictures and/or a list of phrases used often in conversations with your loved one to point to rather than writing the same phrases over and over again. For example, create a photo of a refrigerator with the question, "Are you hungry now?" underneath it.

Be Mindful

Be aware, patient, and kind. If your loved one is tired or not feeling well, his ability to hear that day may be diminished. Be inclusive. Don't go chattering on to others in the room if you realize your care recipient has no idea what you're speaking about. Stop the other conversation, focus on your loved one, and explain slowly and patiently what you've been discussing.

It may take a little more time and effort to speak with the hearing-impaired, but it will be well worth it to reach your goal of meaningful and pleasant communication.

> "Kindness is the language which the deaf can hear and the blind can see."
>
> —Mark Twain, American writer and humorist

COMMUNICATING WITH LOVED ONES WITH MEMORY LOSS

Communication is often one of the first areas affected by memory loss. If your care recipient repeats the same questions or stories too frequently, often searches for the proper word, or has difficulty answering open-ended questions, these could all be early signs of dementia. The Alzheimer's Association defines dementia as a wide range of symptoms associated with a decline in memory or other thinking skills severe enough to reduce a person's ability to perform everyday activities. Alzheimer's disease is the most common type of dementia and is progressive, with symptoms appearing slowly and gradually getting worse. These diagnoses are frightening for the patients and their families to hear, and the fear doesn't disappear for the person diagnosed. It's scary to feel that the world as you know it is slipping away and you can't do things you used to do automatically, such as cooking, driving, or reading.

As a conscious caregiver, you recognize you can't control memory loss, only your reaction to it. The caregiving team for a loved one experiencing memory loss will need to change established language patterns of communication. This is not easy to do and won't happen overnight, because, as mentioned before, how you speak to and interact with family are long-standing habits. The first steps are mindful awareness and a resolve to change. In addition, you should:

- Give short, one-sentence explanations and allow plenty of time for your loved one to process your statement. Repeat instructions *exactly* the same way.
- It's unkind to point out that your loved one forgot whatever or whomever you're discussing. How would you feel if someone repeatedly said to you, "Don't you remember that?!"
- Be flexible and reassuring. As his memories slowly disappear, your loved one will be living more and more in a world of fear. Be responsive to his underlying feelings rather than focusing solely on the actual words he says.
- Don't argue or insist that you're right and she is wrong. Leave the room if necessary to avoid an argument and try again later. Or try

switching to a different topic or activity. And don't take what your loved one says personally even if it's hurtful—it's the disease talking.
- Magnify your patience tenfold to prevent frustration and improve the day-to-day quality of life for everyone. Accept blame when your loved one says you've done something wrong, even if it's not true and in his mind only.

Always remember that a person with memory loss is not *giving* you a hard time; she is *having* a hard time. Put yourself in the other person's place and increase your generosity in everything you say and do.

EXERCISE: Role-Play a Conversation

If you're struggling to put these guidelines into practice, try role-playing a conversation with someone in your life who is not your loved one. This will help you be more conscious and mindful when your loved one is struggling to remember. Here are a couple of sample conversations:

Sample Conversation #1

Dad: "What doctor's appointment? I don't need to see the doctor. There's nothing wrong with me."

Don't Say: "You've been seeing the doctor every three months for the past year. It's written on the calendar, and I told you about it yesterday and this morning." (Don't reason or remind him he forgot.)

Do Say: "It's just a regular checkup. I'm sorry if I forgot to tell you." (Give a short explanation and accept blame even if it's fantasy.)

Sample Conversation #2

Mom: "I can't find my purse. Someone must have stolen it from the house!"

Don't Say: "What? Don't be ridiculous. No one has stolen it. You must have misplaced your purse. Let's look for it." (Don't argue.)

Do Say: "That's a scary thought. I'll make sure the alarm is working properly. Would you help me fold the towels?" (Respond to feelings of anxiety and fear rather than the words. Be reassuring and patient. Distract her with a different subject or activity.)

Learning how to speak with a memory-impaired person takes practice, so have patience with yourself as you learn these new skills. It's hard to break long-entrenched patterns of speaking. Becoming aware of how important the words you choose are and recognizing when to apply them are the first steps toward mindful communication.

CHAPTER SUMMARY

The following are takeaways, action steps, and reminders to help your caregiving journey progress smoothly.

- Being mindful while communicating with your care recipient makes caregiving easier overall. Listening, processing thoughts before you speak, speaking, and nonverbal messages affect your relationship with your loved one. Proceed slowly and kindly when communicating.
- Don't put off difficult conversations with your loved one. Postponing discussions and making decisions about things like driving, moving, and end-of-life wishes won't make it easier and could lead to big problems or a tragedy. Give the topic careful thought by yourself before broaching it with your aging relative and/or caregiving team. Be sure these sensitive conversations take place in a quiet, focused environment, and the participants are not feeling tired, hungry, sick, distracted, or hurried.
- When communicating with a hearing-impaired loved one, keep the overall environment quiet and well lit. Speak slowly and in a normal volume, using short and simple sentences. Shouting will not help.
- When communicating with a person who has memory loss, don't argue, reason, confront, or harp on what she forgot. Instead, give plenty of time for comprehension and a reply. Repeat short and simple sentences. Increase your patience tenfold. Know that your loved one is not *giving* you a hard time; she is *having* a hard time.

CHAPTER 5

Communicating with a Caregiving Team

You've probably heard that "it takes a village" to raise a child. Well, it will take a team to care for your loved one. Naturally, you turn to your closest family (siblings, spouse or significant other, adult children, longtime family friends) first for help in creating a caregiving team. In this chapter, you'll learn how to determine what roles each family member can take and who is best suited to act as the primary caregiver. Suggestions are given about how to hold regular team meetings to keep everyone updated about your loved one's status and discuss decisions about care. You'll also learn how to better communicate with long-distance family caregivers, and how to best connect if *you* are the one living far away. The late stage of life of your loved one brings up many difficult topics that you and your family will have to discuss as well.

CONNECTING WITH SIBLINGS AND EXTENDED FAMILY

The study *Caregiving in the U.S. 2015* reports that only 53 percent of family caregivers say another unpaid caregiver helps their care recipients. When a parent needs care, it is often one adult child who becomes the primary and/or sole caregiver, whether she volunteers for the role or not. The main factors that play a part in determining which sibling steps into the role include gender (more women are caregivers than men), age (it's often the eldest child), and geography (the person who lives the closest). Other factors might include career (more people are working longer) and stage of life (still parenting or with an empty nest).

If you've been chosen as the primary caregiver, be a conscious caregiver as you put together your team. Recognize the need for a team approach in caring for your loved one, so not all of the stress and responsibilities lie on your shoulders alone. You can mindfully decide to make time and space for self-care from the very start by sharing your caregiving journey with people you trust. By creating a safety net of team members, you will feel reassured that if anything should happen to you, there are others who will continue to care for your loved one seamlessly. Also recognize that the more support you have as a caregiver, the less likely you will be to experience chronic stress or burnout.

Open communication among all team members is important in order to provide the best care for your loved one. For example, parents often tell their adult children different things about how they're doing. Keep communication lines open and pool information you each get about your parent's status to get the full picture.

As the primary caregiver, you should ask all other siblings, extended family, neighbors, and trusted friends on your potential caregiving team to do a self-assessment to identify the specific talents or capabilities they can offer. In doing so, *they* will receive an introduction to mindfulness—sitting down in a quiet space to think objectively about their strengths. Have each one make a list to share about how they can best support the team effort. Along with listing their strengths, each person needs to be honest and realistic about how much they *can* do. What are their limits with regard to both time and finances? Considerations about how caregiving might affect their jobs and nuclear families are important and, while they may be hard to predict, are worth thinking over carefully up front.

"The strength of the team is each individual member. The strength of each member is the team."

—Phil Jackson, American basketball coach

Other Potential Team Members

Don't overlook in-laws and children as potential family team members. An aging parent often gets along exceptionally well with a son-in-law or daughter-in-law. Also, children will enjoy helping their grandparents in different ways depending upon their ages. If they're teenagers, they might enjoy driving them on errands. If they're younger, visits from grandchildren can be the highlight of an older person's day. Unless they live near an elementary school or park, seniors can become isolated and rarely glimpse children in their immediate surroundings. Seeing children can bring a great amount of joy, even if no interaction occurs! I still clearly recall visiting my grandparents in their senior living facility and feeling many other residents' eyes on me while I visited with them in the lobby or dining room or out on the boardwalk.

That said, don't be caught off guard if some family members decide not to step up to help. This could be either a negative or a positive, depending upon the existing family dynamics and your care recipient's needs.

Forming a Family Caregiving Team

Adult siblings cooperating to form a caregiving team can be tricky. Every family has a history, and each sibling holds a unique place due to birth order and personality. Family members developed ways of communicating with each other over long periods of time, and these patterns might still exist, even if you haven't been close since childhood.

Old family dynamics, sibling rivalries, and prior disagreements don't always vanish because a parent needs care.

When families get together, people tend to slip into their old roles. Maybe your older brother was the responsible one, your younger sister was the baby, and you were the sensitive middle child. Notice whether you're falling back into these same family places even though you're all adults now. It's time you all adapt your old childhood roles to who you are today in this caregiving stage of life. For example, if you think your sister is less capable because she's always been the baby of the family, you may be less likely to ask for help from her. If you approach her differently, she may prove to be more helpful than you ever imagined she could be.

Be aware that stress can trigger disruptive family patterns, and try not to fall into this trap. When old needs well up, such as wanting the love and approval of your parents, it can trigger sibling rivalry. If this happens, keep your emotions in check and stay focused on the number one priority: your loved one's care. It's not about which child your parent loves the best or which of you knows more about what he wants. If there's not an emergency, allow some time for everyone to get on the same page. It's natural for each team member to adjust to the new situation and dynamics in her own way and time.

Hold Family Meetings

In the previous chapter you learned how to use mindful communication to make sure your loved one participates in his or her care if possible, and you know that you should discuss any potential issues before they come to fruition in order to have a plan in place. In that vein, before a crisis happens, your family team should sit down together with your loved one to discuss the "what ifs." Choices and decisions are better when made in a calm and proactive, rather than reactive, state.

Your loved one should be an active participant in all discussions and decisions as long as his or her cognitive abilities allow. Even when partial decline prevents his full participation, you can still include him in family meetings. If there are topics you need to discuss that could hurt, upset, or agitate him, hold a separate meeting beforehand or afterward with just the caregiving team to cover those particular issues.

The first family meeting ideally will be held in person, and the meetings will continue at regular intervals via phone or Internet with long-distance family team members. The timing of these meetings will depend on your loved one's health and current needs, but connecting every one to three months as a start is recommended. At the first meeting, decide jointly how often to have family meetings and mark them all on the calendar then for the coming year.

Encourage everyone to keep a list of questions and concerns that arise in between meetings. One family member should be responsible for creating an agenda and sending it out to everyone a few days before the next meeting date. Others can then add their questions to the agenda. The person acting as health advocate for your loved one (most likely the primary caregiver) should share all medical updates in between meetings too. We'll discuss health advocacy later on in Chapter 6, but for now, know that everyone needs to stay in the loop about your loved one's health status.

Being a conscious caregiver and also the primary one, you know to proceed with caution and are probably more aware of and sensitive to your care recipient's feelings than other team members. Notice the degree to which your loved one participates in the family meetings. Talk about the meetings with him one-on-one afterward, and get *his* perspective and assessment about how helpful they are. Some elderly parents may not want a fuss made over them, so perhaps they don't need to be at every meeting. Other parents would feel left out if they weren't invited. Some may ask you not to discuss certain private matters with the whole group. Listen carefully to the feedback your loved one gives and adjust accordingly. If you've met as a team to discuss something without your loved one, since you are the primary caregiver, you should meet with him alone and share what was discussed and what the team tentatively decided. From there, you may need to have a series of conversations about the topic if it's a difficult one. For example, have another few talks with your father one-on-one, followed by a phone conversation with your brother who lives out of state, and then all together in person when the family is gathered for a visit. Don't ever ruin a holiday or special occasion by discussing serious or upsetting things on that day.

"To effectively communicate, we must realize that we are all different in the way we perceive the world and use this understanding as a guide to our communication with others."

—Tony Robbins, motivational speaker and writer

LONG-DISTANCE CAREGIVING

Multigenerational families used to live within the same town, block, or even house, but this is rare in our society these days. Career and lifestyle choices have spread many families across the country. As a result, long-distance caregiving is becoming more common and may be something that you deal with when your loved one needs help. Practicing mindfulness is especially important when you're a caregiver living far away, because you need to be focused and tuned in even more when you can't see your loved one often. For starters, listening extra carefully during phone conversations is vital, not only to hear her words but also to read between the lines and understand the unsaid message.

Long-distance caregiving typically occurs in one of three formats:

1. You're the primary caregiver for your loved one from a distance of thirty to three thousand plus miles away. Anyone living at least an hour away is considered a long-distance caregiver.
2. You live far away but assist the primary caregiver, who lives near your care recipient.
3. You and several family members all live far away from your loved one and coordinate care remotely.

Your responsibilities will vary greatly depending upon which of these scenarios exists. The good news is that a long-distance caregiver can be helpful no matter how far away.

Thanks to technology, there are easier ways to communicate and accomplish many tasks, so take full advantage of it. Even if you don't live nearby you can research information and resources; order medications or medical equipment; shop for just about anything and have it delivered; have an online visit via Skype, FaceTime, or the WhatsApp Messenger; find community services; arrange transportation; arrange meal and/or grocery deliveries; communicate with medical personnel; manage finances and insurance; and meet with anyone local to you who is involved in your loved one's care. As technology advances, there will be even more online options to utilize for caregiving.

Let's take a look at some scenarios for each of the long-distance caregiving options:

If You Are the Sole Primary Caregiver from Afar

While it might take extra planning and organization, being a long-distance primary caregiver is manageable. Realize that your loved one may not want to ask for help from you or anyone, so you might need to do some investigating to figure out what his needs really are. Does he just need a little help with a few chores, or is it time to consider hiring non-medical home care or home health aides for several hours a week? It's easier for people to appear to be functioning normally and hide problems if you only speak with them by phone or have short visits. Arrange to spend at least a long weekend with your loved one a minimum of once every three months and be alert for warning signs that all may not be as it seems on the surface (we'll discuss this further in Chapter 6).

CONSCIOUS CONNECTIONS

Keep in mind that long-married couples are very good at "covering" for each other's weaknesses or deficits. Their daily behaviors, such as cooking, grocery shopping, and cleaning up around their home, are most likely done in partnership subconsciously, because their teamwork has evolved over a long time. Many adult children don't know one parent has dementia or is declining in other ways until the other parent is in the hospital. Then the children see quickly how the parent at home can't safely function on his or her own any longer.

Watch for Signs of Decline

Throughout your visit keep your eyes and ears open for possible signs of decline in your loved one's physical or cognitive abilities. Observe your care recipient subtly and quietly as she does everyday actions. Watch how she performs activities of daily living (ADL), and make mental notes to yourself of any assistance that might be needed.

It's best to be honest and let your loved one know that you're making these observations, but don't make him feel that you are "spying." Be as unobtrusive and sensitive as possible while you assess. Also notice the condition of your loved one's home and car(s). Are they being kept in good condition, both the interior and exterior? Before talking with your loved one about any observations, think about possible solutions and then approach him with a win-win goal in mind. You're not trying to take away your loved one's independence or change his life drastically (unless it's a matter of safety). You're there to help support his lifestyle for as long as possible.

Connect with Their Existing Network

During your visit connect with your loved one's friends, neighbors, and doctors to exchange contact information. With your loved one's permission, ask if you might keep in touch with this group of people periodically, to ensure that everything is going okay. You might have your loved one exchange house keys with a neighbor or friend living close by in case of emergency. Go to all doctor's appointments with her during your visits, and ask your loved one to complete a medical release form allowing the doctors to release health information to you. If your loved one is reluctant to share personal information with you or other family members, remind her that this is for use only in case of an emergency and that you will respect her privacy and confidentiality.

Then be sure you follow up regularly with the contacts you've made. Most people will understand and be happy to help an older adult if there is no family living nearby. Be alert for calls from anyone in this group too. If a neighbor, friend, extended family member, or medical person calls you with a concern after you're back home, take this input seriously and investigate further.

Take Care of Safety Concerns

Once you and your loved one agree on what is needed, take care of the most important priorities first, which are those concerning his or her safety. For example, if a certain room in your care recipient's home appears dimly lit, get brighter bulbs, buy new overhead lights, or add lamps. If there is a step outside, put bright fluorescent tape on the edge to call attention to it.

Don't pressure yourself to get everything done in one trip. If you can't do it all, either plan another trip in the near future to finish up or connect with services in the area and communicate with them once you're home. It can help to do some online research and speak with your loved one before your arrival to get his input on where he could use help. It's important to make time for fun with your loved one during your visit and not make it only a "caregiving business trip." The time you have together is precious, so keep making memories.

Call in Help

If circumstances keep you from visiting regularly, or your loved one's needs become too challenging to handle long-distance, consider hiring a geriatric care manager (also known as an aging life care professional). This person may be a social worker, nurse, gerontologist, psychologist, or other professional who is trained to provide assistance for your loved one and your family by coordinating needed care and services in the area in which your care recipient lives. While especially helpful for long-distance caregivers, geriatric care managers can be hired by any family caregivers in need. This person will become an advocate for your care recipient and for you.

After care arrangements are in place the geriatric care manager regularly visits your loved one. She should do frequent reevaluations to monitor and adjust care as things change. Her assistance will definitely save you time and possibly money, too, since you won't have to make as many trips to check on your loved one. Services are billed privately on a fee-for-service basis. Currently, neither Medicare nor Medicaid recognizes geriatric care management as a billable service. In addition, delegating multiple caregiving responsibilities to a care manager will reduce your stress level and help keep you from feeling overwhelmed. Remember, taking care of yourself is a big part of conscious caregiving, so be sure to find professional help if and when you need it.

If You Are Assisting the Primary Caregiver, Who Lives Near Your Loved One

If you live far away from your loved one, you might feel an added layer of guilt because you aren't there to offer hands-on help, you wish you could do more, or you wish you lived closer. It's perfectly normal to feel this way, but don't undervalue your contributions to the family team effort. If you live so far away that visiting isn't a realistic option, try to be present at family meetings (even if only by phone or online) in order to remain involved and communicate with the caregiving team. Emails, phone calls, and texts in between meetings will also help you stay connected. As you'll see in the following sections, your role as a long-distance caregiver is valued and very important.

Employ Mindful Listening

Often a long-distance caregiver serves as the person the primary caregiver vents to, so put what you learned about mindful listening in the previous chapter to work and consciously focus on being a good listener and provide emotional support. Listening—really listening—is a powerful resource. Be a "safe place" where a primary caregiver can say whatever's on his mind without being judged and know the conversation will be kept confidential.

Ask. Then Ask Again.

Ask the primary caregiver what you can do from afar, get it done, and then ask what else you can do. Keep asking, even if the primary caregiver is reluctant initially to assign you tasks. He may need to get accustomed to accepting help from you if you've recently entered the picture, or he may not realize how many things you can accomplish remotely. The primary caregiver will definitely need your ongoing support over time, even if not continuously. Keep making it clear that you are a willing care participant.

CONSCIOUS CONNECTIONS

Don't fall into the trap of making your visit all business. Be sure to build in fun times all together with your loved one, as well as enjoyable activities you and the primary caregiver do alone. For example, maybe you make time to visit new or unusual restaurants for lunch in your mother's town when you're out doing caregiving errands together for her.

Brainstorm helpful solutions together and offer to do online research. Perhaps you can be the one to research, have introductory calls with, and narrow down the choices of estate planning attorneys in your parent's city and discuss which to hire at the next family meeting. Attend a general caregiving support group in your area or one specific to your loved one's disease if he has a diagnosis.

Visit Regularly

Visit as regularly as possible and give the primary caregiver the best gift you can—a break. Offer her either 100 percent respite, if she wants to go away on a vacation, or partial respite, if she has a pressing work project or home improvement job to complete. For example, let her take a break while you visit with your loved one between lunch and dinner every afternoon during your time there. Let her know you understand and appreciate her role. If the primary caregiver is a support group member, attend a meeting with her during your visit. In doing so, you may learn more about your loved one's diagnosis or hear new caregiving techniques. More importantly, it shows the primary caregiver that you endorse and value the self-care she is doing by being a support group member.

All of this said, it's important to note that visiting periodically can be a double-edged sword. Remember, you are only getting a "snapshot" of your loved one's daily existence. Resist the urge to swoop in, make assessments, proclaim you see new issues that need "fixing," and expect big changes to be made quickly as a result of your input. Long-distance caregivers often push their agendas in order to make their impact felt during a visit, but they could be off base or out of line. On the flip side, you might very well notice certain issues the primary caregiver doesn't see due to his close proximity to your loved one. Looking at living situations with a fresh set of eyes can be helpful. So keep this in mind and remain open *and* cautious simultaneously.

If you've been having regular family meetings, review the overall care plan goals you've agreed on and begin discussions using those as a guide. After you've talked through any issues and come to a mutual understanding, then you can discuss plans with your loved one if and when appropriate.

CASE STUDY: Patti, Cathy, Jane, and Long-Distance Caregiving

Patti was the primary caregiver for her mom, Jane, who lived in an assisted living community just a mile and a half away from Patti's home. Her sister, Cathy, lived in another state and was the long-distance caregiver. Patti describes how they coordinated caring for their mom:

"We were always very close, and we talked a lot by phone. Cathy would call my mom as much as she could. She is also a letter writer, so she would send Mom cards and letters and was outstanding in that way. She was as hands-on as she could be from a distance. When she would come for a visit, I would let her do the bulk of the caregiving responsibilities. I would go over every once in a while with her to my mom's to visit, but mainly I'd let her have that one-on-one time, because I could easily take over and I didn't want to do that. To Cathy's credit, she quickly learned the names of the staff and got into the groove of the community. She learned the staff's names, had a great memory for that, and they all got to know her too. When she was here, she was really here, and it was a huge plus."

Patti's husband, Paul, another member of their family caregiving team, explains his observation of Cathy's visits:

"One interesting phenomenon that took place was when Cathy would come down to visit two or three times a year, she would try to make up for all the time she wasn't here. She would be with her for six or seven hours at a time, which was overwhelming for someone with dementia. We all understood where she was coming from. But, since she was only here for a week's visit, it was hard for Cathy to pull back and not see Mom. After Cathy would leave, it took Mom a couple of days to get back on an even keel."

If you are the primary caregiver and a long-distance caregiver visits, keep in mind this possible perspective. You may have your own particular caregiving "routine," which will likely get disrupted during the person's visit. Please be gracious and welcoming to the long-distance caregiver, not resentful of his or her "intrusion" or defensive when she offers feedback or suggestions about care.

If You All Live Apart from Your Loved One

This situation is similar to being the solo primary caregiver from afar, but you have family team members to coordinate with and share the tasks and responsibilities. This can be both a plus and a minus. One person isn't overwhelmed by caregiving, but it may be a challenge for you as the primary caregiver to keep everyone updated constantly. As a conscious caregiver, stop to think through the best ways to keep everyone connected, updated, and engaged in caregiving while you're all living apart, and possibly at great distances. Also give careful consideration to useful strategies to assess how your loved one is doing from afar and how other team members can be involved in this information gathering. Thanks to technology, orchestrating the team's efforts is much easier.

Assess Strengths and Weaknesses

As with the long-distance caregiving situations mentioned earlier in this chapter, be sure to assess everyone's strengths and weaknesses and select duties that make the most sense for each of you. Communicate regularly with each other about your questions and concerns. Visits can be made individually or all together, depending upon your care recipient's needs. For example, you may visit your loved one alone to complete difficult household chores, such as cleaning the leaves out of rain gutters or shoring up a fence blown over in a storm. But if your loved one has received a serous medical diagnosis, all family team members may want to coordinate their visit to meet with your loved one and her doctor all together. After a solo visit, be sure to update the others about what you saw, address any new needs that have arisen, and adjust the care plan if necessary.

Plan Ahead

Just like all parts of your caregiving journey, there is no crystal ball. Long-distance caregiving may last as long as your loved one lives, or it may be for only a brief period of time. If multiple family caregivers are involved, plan ahead in case your loved one needs to move near a different caregiver, or one of you needs to move in with her, either temporarily or permanently. Again, it's better to be prepared than to have to decide and make these large life changes quickly in a crisis situation.

EXERCISE: Figure Out Where Your Loved One Will Move

If you and your family members are all taking care of your loved one from a distance, you may find yourselves having to make a decision as to where your loved one will live if she has to move out of her home. All members of the caregiving team should ask themselves the following questions before you jointly make a decision. Don't just think about the present; answer these questions with a loved one's likely future decline in mind:

- Can my home (house, condominium, or apartment) safely accommodate Mom's needs? For example, are there stairs inside and outside she would need to use regularly? Would it be possible to add ramps if needed to navigate them in the future?
- Is there a separate bedroom that would become hers? Is there a bathroom that she can use attached or close to it? Can that bathroom be retrofitted to make it safer over time (e.g., would she have to climb into a tub, or is there a separate shower stall to step into easily, and is there room for a shower chair)?
- Will our lifestyles mesh? Is she a night owl who likes to sleep in versus our family, who are all early risers? How will she do around my teens and their friends? Will she want to cook her own foods, is she on a special diet, or can she eat the items on our regular family menu?
- Are her doctors close enough to us, or will we have to locate new doctors? How far away is the closest hospital?
- Are there senior recreation facilities (senior centers, programs through my city's parks and recreation department) that will be of interest? Where else she can socialize?
- How will she get around? Will she be able to use public transportation when/if she can no longer drive? Does our garage or driveway have room for her car?
- Is there a church or temple nearby she may be interested in attending for religious services and social events? How will she get there if we aren't able to attend?
- Can she stay occupied all day safely and contentedly while we are at work and/or school?
- If her health needs change, who in my family will be available to provide care, both short and long term?

- You may want to add other questions, depending upon your family's particular circumstances and location. For example, should any of the adult children consider moving in with Mom? Or can she rotate homes, spending a few months with each sibling?

After you've each answered the questions, find a way to come together as a group and discuss your answers to determine which location makes the most sense for your loved one to move to. There may not be a perfect option, but try to have as many pluses and as few minuses as possible on the list. And be sure to get detailed input from your loved one about this life-altering decision.

CHAPTER SUMMARY

The following are takeaways, action steps, and reminders to help your caregiving journey progress smoothly.

- The primary caregiver is usually a spouse or the oldest, female adult child who lives closest geographically. The primary caregiver may live far away, but much can be accomplished from a distance, along with regular visits.
- Creating a family caregiving team is vital for sharing responsibilities and keeping stress levels lower. Close family members and trusted friends can self-assess to determine their capabilities as well as availability for tasks to be done.
- Long-distance team members can be active participants in a myriad of ways. The perspectives on your loved one gained from members living close by as well as far away are all valid and should be considered when formulating a care plan.
- Don't fall into outmoded or hurtful family patterns of speaking during a stressful time.
- Regularly scheduled family meetings allow communication to continue over time and in different geographic locations. Mark them on a shared calendar for a year in advance, and then attend (in person or online) with input about your loved one after a visit, care suggestions, and completed assignments done for the team. Plan solo visits or coordinate group visits if you all live far away from your loved one in order to check in.

CHAPTER 6

Being an Advocate for Your Loved One . . . and Yourself

Part of your responsibility as a family caregiver is speaking up and taking action for your loved one when she is unable to do so. This role begins during routine doctor visits and while deciding who you and your loved one want to be part of your caregiving medical team. Your role as advocate becomes larger when your loved one is admitted to a hospital or skilled nursing facility (SNF). In this chapter, you'll learn how to be the best conscious advocate you can be, how to make a medical stay more palatable for your loved one, how to best communicate with medical providers, and how to take care of yourself during these stressful times. You'll also learn how to make your loved one's transition home as smooth as possible.

BEING AN ADVOCATE FOR YOUR LOVED ONE

Being an advocate for your loved one continues through all phases of caregiving and consists of three parts:

1. Educating yourself
2. Speaking up
3. Taking actions on your loved one's behalf

If your care recipient is "aging in place" (continuing to live in his own home while aging), you will first need to be on your toes to work around any new obstacles encountered in his daily routine. Then explore creative ways to solve any issues so your loved one can remain living safely at home. And if and when he moves into a new senior care community, your antennae must stay up to notice ways to smooth out any bumps in the road encountered there. When health issues crop up, you'll want to learn as much as you can about the condition so you can maximize the results from doctors' visits, lab tests, or surgeries. Helping your loved one navigate through our increasingly complex health care system is a large part of being an advocate.

CREATING YOUR CAREGIVING MEDICAL TEAM

Being a health care advocate is often the first caregiving responsibility family caregivers take on—usually when your loved one is living independently and doesn't need any other assistance. If your care recipient already sees a primary care physician (PCP) regularly, start going to these doctor visits with him now for two reasons:

1. To get to know the PCP and her staff
2. To become a second set of eyes and ears for your loved one

As your loved one's advocate, you may provide input for the doctor, respectfully and with the permission of your loved one. For example, you'll be the one who updates the doctor about any emergency room visits, medication changes, or visits with new specialists your care recipient forgets to mention. You'll also remind your loved one about any questions he wants answered before the doctor finishes up the examination.

You become your loved one's second set of ears during a doctor visit. Write detailed notes about everything the doctor tells you at each visit (even if it's a regular checkup), especially if your loved one is showing any early signs of hearing or memory loss. These notes can be used for your own reference and to remind your loved one what the doctor's instructions were. If you or your loved one aren't clear about something the doctor says or prescribes, ask her to repeat it for you both. And don't hesitate to ask for online resources and/or handouts about health issues discussed during the visit.

EXERCISE: Start a Medical Health Journal

Start a medical health journal with and for your care recipient. This is where to record the date and notes taken after visits to every doctor, dentist, and other medical care provider. Write your care recipient's personal information in one section, such as Social Security and Medicare numbers. Include information about any secondary insurance or long-term care insurance policies he has.

Include a page with complete contact information for all doctors and health care providers your loved one sees. Indicate which is the preferred way to communicate with each: telephone, email, and/or text.

As a result of the Health Insurance Portability and Accountability Act (HIPAA), patient care paperwork includes a privacy release form listing who, in addition to the patient, should be made privy to medical issues, test results, and treatment options. Encourage your loved one to include all family caregivers on the authorization, including those living nearby and those far away. Put copies of the signed form in the medical health journal.

List your loved one's medical conditions and any allergies or other special medical information, such as if he has a pacemaker. Write down all medications taken (prescription, over-the-counter, and herbal), strength, dosages, side effects experienced, and how long he will be taking them. Include complete contact information for his or her preferred pharmacy.

If your loved one is diagnosed with a chronic or life-threatening illness, keep an overall timeline of medical events from diagnosis on, including treatments received and those scheduled for the future. Also record all related tests and lab work done, with all results received.

Help your loved one complete a durable power of attorney for health care (also known as an advance directive) to include in the journal. This legal document appoints a trusted person, called a health care proxy or health care power of attorney, to be his or her agent to make any necessary health care decisions. The appointed health care proxy must follow the medical treatments and/or life-sustaining measures written in this document in the event that the care recipient can't speak for herself. Usually the primary family caregiver is given these powers.

There is a new form called Physician's Orders for Life-Sustaining Treatment (POLST) that translates a patient's wishes into detailed medical orders that go beyond the content in an advance directive. The POLST document is geared toward those with serious illnesses or who are close to the end of their life. Your loved one and her physician sign it after detailed discussions about your loved one's wishes, health care goals, and desired treatments. Family disputes about health issues can be avoided if your care recipient has documented her end-of-life wishes in these legal documents. It is never too early to have them completed and executed.

Who's on the Team?

As your loved one ages, you may encourage him to see a geriatrician, a physician who specializes in treating the health issues of older adults. Other specialists you might want on your team are a dentist, optometrist and/or ophthalmologist, cardiologist, neurologist, and any other doctors who specialize in your loved one's health conditions. Mobile dentists are able to go beyond teeth cleaning and basic checkups and can perform extractions and root canals on residents living in assisted living communities.

Physician's Assistant and Nurse

A physician's assistant (PA) is a nationally certified and state-licensed medical professional. PAs can be found working independently or in health care groups with physicians and other providers. They undergo rigorous medical training in order to become licensed and certified to diagnose, treat, and prescribe medicine. They have a foundation in primary care but, over the course of their careers, may come to specialize in the field of geriatrics. Depending upon the setting and the skill level required, nurse practitioners may have the following designations: registered nurse (RN), licensed vocational nurse (LVN), licensed practical nurse (LPN), or certified nurse's assistant (CNA).

Occupational and Physical Therapist

Your loved one may also need the services of an occupational therapist (OT) and/or physical therapist (PT), especially after a hospitalization. Occupational therapists help older adults overcome physical challenges and enable them to return to their home life, including activities of daily living (ADLs) such as dressing, grooming, cooking, and eating. Physical therapists focus on improving a person's mobility and are more likely to treat physical recovery. There is a synergy between OT and PT, which is why they are often prescribed together by a referring doctor. For example, if your loved one breaks her arm, the physical therapist will focus on regaining complete use and mobility of the arm, hand, and elbow. The occupational therapist will work with your loved one on using eating utensils, brushing her teeth, and combing her hair. Both may offer tips to make your loved one's living environment safer and easier to navigate via home improvements and the use of adaptive equipment, such as a walker.

CONSCIOUS CONNECTIONS

Sixty percent of people with dementia are at risk for wandering or getting lost. The MedicAlert Foundation and the Alzheimer's Association have teamed up to form the Safe Return program, a nationwide emergency response service for people with Alzheimer's disease and other related forms of dementia. Safe Return works to reunite the person with a family member or caregiver through a 24/7 network of community support, including local law enforcement agencies and the Alzheimer's Association.

Social Worker

Social workers help people solve or cope with some of life's most difficult challenges and clinically trained social workers also provide diagnoses and treatment of mental health issues. A social worker, psychiatrist, or psychologist who specializes in eldercare can address the mental health of your loved one and/or anyone on your family caregiving team throughout your caregiving years. Mental health is as important as physical health. The possibility of experiencing depression exists throughout the caregiving years, so don't overlook the contribution these professionals can make to a better quality of life for yourself and your loved one.

COMMUNICATING WITH DOCTORS AND MEDICAL STAFF

Thanks to technology, more doctors and health care providers now communicate via email and texting. Many medical offices offer free online patient portals to send and receive questions and answers, view test results, request prescription refills, confirm upcoming appointments, and view electronic health records. Ask doctors about their preferences for communicating between appointments.

Efficiently planned communication with health care providers allows you to be a better advocate. In advance of any discussion, think about what you will ask or tell the doctor. If you're upset, first take time to pause, then think. Connect again later on when you're calmer, with an understanding of what upset you and why, and what the ultimate goal is. Knee-jerk, reactive conversations are generally not productive ones.

Family caregivers can obtain proxy access to connect to their loved ones' online health records. Your care recipient will need to complete an adult proxy consent form and submit it to the doctor's office in order to gain access. This is an efficient way to keep long-distance caregivers up-to-date on medical information. You can make sure you are consciously communicating with your loved one's doctors by doing the following as well:

What to Bring

Before you go with your loved one to any medical appointment, write down a list of questions or concerns all of you have, including those from long-distance caregivers. If possible, don't make the list in haste the day of the appointment. Keep a running list of questions that arise in between visits. Prioritize the list before you go, putting the most important questions first. Bring a pad and pen to write down the answers you get during the appointment; these will become part of the medical health journal you've created.

Bring all health insurance information and the list from your medical health journal that includes all drug prescriptions, vitamins, herbs, and supplements your loved one takes to every medical appointment so each provider has full knowledge of what she is currently taking, the dosage, and the schedule.

Respect Your Loved One

As long as your loved one is cognitively able, allow the conversation to flow between the doctor and your care recipient. Pay attention to see if the doctor is carefully and respectfully listening and responding to your loved one's concerns. Sometimes a doctor will ask for your input, but steer the conversation back to the two of them if you notice the doctor speaking more with you than with your care recipient. If the doctor isn't listening to your loved one, or if you feel he is hurrying in any way, you may want to speak with your loved one later about changing doctors. It's rude and disrespectful for a doctor, nurse, or any medical practitioner to speak at length about your care recipient as if she is not present. Be mindful of your loved one, and think about how that would make you feel.

In addition to focusing the appointment on your loved one, be sure to preserve your loved one's privacy and dignity by leaving the room if she asks you to do so during an examination. The doctor may also be more comfortable one-on-one and engage more attentively with your loved one during that time.

Communicate with the Doctor

Never be afraid to ask your loved one's doctor a lot of questions. Don't hesitate to ask a doctor to spell out or further explain a term, test, or treatment you or your care recipient may not understand. For example, say, "Can you explain it in a different way? I don't understand." Before leaving an appointment, make sure all information and instructions are completely understood by you and your loved one.

Another key to communicating with doctors and medical staff is to use your calendar and schedule a time to follow up with them to ensure you receive responses in a timely manner. Don't be hesitant to contact the office as an advocate for your loved one if the deadline passes, but do so calmly and cordially.

Speak to the Doctor Privately

If you have concerns or input about your care recipient's health and do not want to speak with the doctor about that particular worry in his or her presence, call the office a few days before the scheduled appointment and ask to speak with the doctor privately. Medical professionals are used to families making such requests, and you can do this either through an advance phone consultation or by arranging to discretely speak to the doctor during an appointment if permission has been granted via the privacy release form. For example, you may be concerned about your loved one's emotional state ("Can you ask Mom if she's feeling overly sad or depressed?"), or he may be showing signs of memory loss ("Can you please test Dad's cognition level as part of your exam?"). By discussing these concerns privately with the doctor first, you preserve your loved one's dignity and avoid causing alarm in case your observations are incorrect.

Seniors often hold doctors in high esteem and will listen willingly and respectfully to them about an issue before they'll listen to you about the same topic. Use this to your advantage and privately ask your doctor in advance to raise important issues with your loved one during the exam. For example, you might ask the doctor to discuss cutting back on driving or getting part-time paid care at home. These topics will likely be more palatable if your loved one hears them addressed initially and/or reinforced by his doctor. After the doctor raises the subject, you can give your input and then continue that discussion after the appointment with your loved one and your family caregiving team.

HOSPITALIZATIONS AND SKILLED NURSING FACILITY STAYS

At some time in your caregiving experience, your loved one could end up in the emergency room (ER) and/or be admitted to the hospital. After hospitalization many patients spend extended time in a skilled nursing facility (SNF) for rehabilitation before they transition back to their homes.

While in the hospital or a skilled nursing facility your care recipient is not at her strongest, physically or cognitively; therefore, looking out for her best interests is more critical during these times. Your role as patient advocate means listening carefully, observing, and speaking up for your loved one. However, as long as she has the ability to comprehend and participate in health care decisions, include her in the discussions. Even when feeling ill, your loved one still has the right to listen to the conversations and give input.

Be a technical interpreter, the person who helps doctors, nurses, and other providers explain medical jargon when necessary. Make notes about what the doctors and nurses have said in the medical health journal each time you have a significant conversation. Then write down follow-up questions as you, others on your family team, and your loved one think of them, so you will be sure not to forget them. Be persistent in getting all of your questions answered fully and clearly.

> "Promise me you'll always remember: You're braver than you believe, and stronger than you seem, and smarter than you think."
>
> —A.A. Milne, British author

Be Your Care Recipient's Voice

Be the person who helps your care recipient fully explain his or her situation to the doctors, nurses, and other staff. This goes beyond medical history and current condition; it includes the everyday things, such as suggesting the nurses speak slowly so your hearing-impaired care recipient can read their lips. Or letting them know his glasses are for distance, not for reading. Or mentioning that she prefers applesauce instead of water for swallowing medications. These are small yet significant personal preferences your loved one may not think to express when he is not feeling well. The little things matter.

If you're unhappy with something that occurs or have a complaint, speak up in an assertive yet civil manner, away from your care recipient. You don't need to add unnecessary upset to your care recipient's world by letting her hear you complain. Also, approaching hospital or skilled nursing staff politely will yield a better result than being unpleasant or aggressive. An old adage applies here: "You get more flies with honey than with vinegar."

CONSCIOUS CONNECTIONS

Practice mindfulness techniques to remain calm, especially in front of your loved one, because she can pick up on your level of anxiety. If you seem calm (at least on the outside), she won't be as frightened. If your loved one senses that you are upset, she will become more anxious. Remember, deep breathing can be done anywhere.

Have Someone Be There

Depending upon your loved one's medical condition, your other responsibilities, and finances, you may want to consider hiring a companion or nurse's aide through a professional caregiving agency to spend time with your loved one when you or other family caregivers can't be there. Older adults may decline in their normal level of functioning or become confused while in an unfamiliar environment, so having someone with them, especially during the night, may help greatly. Or, if you have a larger family caregiving team, set up a schedule so that each person can be at the hospital or skilled nursing facility for a particular "shift."

Know the Staff

If you don't already know all of the doctors treating your loved one, find out from the nurses when they will be making rounds and go out of your way to be there to introduce yourself, even if it's early in the morning or late at night. If that's not possible, get the doctor's phone number and ask questions by phone. In our world of electronic, remote communication, face-to-face conversations about a loved one's health care are still preferable, and the medical professional will be more likely to remember you if you meet in person.

Also get to know the nurses caring for your loved one. Introduce yourself, your loved one, and any other visiting family members. Appreciation goes a long way, so thank them for the hard work they're doing. Ask the nurses, too, what the preferred way is to reach them with questions or to get help in your loved one's room so you don't become a pest. What direct phone number should you call to get an update from them on days you're not there, and what number should long-distance and other family members call? Ask what things you can do to help them, as long as it is safe for you and your loved one, such as going for a walk together around the hospital floor or skilled nursing facility.

CONSCIOUS CONNECTIONS

On the day of discharge or shortly thereafter, bring or send a basket of fruit, cookies, healthy snacks, or whatever treat you think the staff will like, along with a thank-you note. If you have casual conversations with them during your loved one's stay, you might get an idea of what they'd enjoy as a group gift.

MAKING THE TRANSITION HOME

You are given between a few days' and a week's notice before your loved one is discharged from the hospital or skilled nursing facility. Use that time to to prepare so the transition goes more smoothly. Thoughtful planning can prevent or at least alleviate stressful or unsafe situations from occurring. As advocate and primary caregiver, you know your loved one's current home and lifestyle in depth and are in the best position to analyze and discuss the transition home with the medical staff. The health facility staff are swamped with patients and won't have time to help in the transition beyond completing the discharge process. That's where you come in.

Set Up Medical Equipment

Anticipate any new medical equipment your loved one will need and where it will fit into her environment, whether she is living independently at home or in an assisted living facility. For example, will the wheelchair fit through all the doorways (the entrance and all rooms)? Will she need a hospital bed? Coordinate with the discharge social worker in the hospital or skilled nursing facility to ensure that it's ordered, delivered, and set up at home before discharge. Test to be sure all electric features of the medical equipment are working properly. For example, do the bed's head and feet areas move up and down when the buttons are pressed? Will your loved one need a temporary commode set up near the bed? Will she be able to get to the kitchen or dining room to eat, or should you provide a tray for eating in bed? Will ramps need to be added at the entryway or inside to accommodate a wheelchair? Make the necessary modifications based on whether they're expected to be temporary or permanent—which is sometimes hard to predict. Make decisions based on the best information you have at the time, and pay attention to details.

Get Clear Instructions

Meet with the doctor, nurses, and physical and occupational therapists to get clear written and verbal instructions your care recipient will need to follow once at home. Also ask how long each of the instructions will need to be followed. Is it only until a check-in with the doctor in a few days or weeks, or could it be months until she is fully recovered? No one has a crystal ball, but the medical professionals should be able to give you an idea based on their experience with other older adults.

If possible, attend physical and/or occupational therapy sessions before your care recipient is discharged. The more information you absorb about what his or her physical needs will be at home, the better. Watching a live therapy session is a better way of learning than simply having a therapist tell you or show you via diagrams what they're doing. They will probably have you "practice" exercises or techniques with your loved one during a session to be sure you both understand and can do them on your own. You can also use your mobile phone to videotape the exercises as they're doing them.

CASE STUDY: Linda and Rehabilitation

At age ninety-five my dad fell and had surgery to replace a broken hip. He spent one week in the hospital recuperating and the following two more weeks in a rehabilitation facility. We were ecstatic when he was told he was being released and could go back to the apartment in the assisted living community.

Life quickly became more challenging when the rehabilitation nurse handed me a 38-page manual covering the basics of post-operative home care for hip-replacement patients. I had to examine many facets of my dad's daily living from a new perspective. The manual included precautions, exercises, transfer techniques (i.e., getting in and out of bed, cars, and chairs), and best practices for using a walker, stair climbing (thankfully he didn't have to navigate any stairs), dressing, and bathing.

Having these detailed instructions guided me through an assessment of how my dad's life would be at home after discharge. I was able to think through things such as which car would be the easiest for him to get in and out of and how he would put on his socks and shoes every morning without breaking the post-op rules for hip-replacement patients. Conscious caregiving is often found in the details.

Hospitals and rehabilitation facility staff will review verbally and provide written instructions about all medications with the patient and their family at discharge. Be sure you, as primary caregiver, are present for this, because your care recipient may be weak or unable to concentrate fully. Be clear about the names of all medications, what they are for, dosages, and when they are taken. Are there any special instructions, such as a medication that must be taken on an empty stomach or, the opposite, taken with food? Know exactly which medicines were already given to your loved one on the day of discharge to prevent double doses. Request that a nurse call, email, or fax any prescriptions to the preferred pharmacy before discharge. You can then pick them up on the way home.

Arrange a Schedule

When your loved one first gets home she may be very happy and relieved but weak and/or slightly disoriented from his or her medical ordeal. Just as when she was in the hospital or skilled nursing facility, arrange for extra care if needed. Advocate for your loved one by arranging for other family members, friends, and/or neighbors to spend the first few days post-discharge with your care recipient when you, the primary caregiver, can't be there. Then cut back on the additional help little by little, until your loved one can live safely on his own again.

> "The greatest weapon against stress is our ability to choose one thought over another."
>
> —William James, American psychologist

TAKE A STEP BACK AND CHECK IN WITH YOURSELF

Self-care is so important during this time period because caregiving is even more intense when you're busy running to a hospital or skilled nursing facility, then settling your loved one back at home or moving her to a completely new living situation. You don't want to run yourself ragged and risk ending up in the hospital yourself. You know your loved one is in a safe place while in the hospital or skilled nursing facility, so give yourself a well-earned break now by using the ideas in the following exercise.

EXERCISE: Check In and Carve Out Some "Me Time"

You shouldn't feel bad about wanting to feel good. If you haven't carved out "me time" recently, begin again right now—even for just five minutes. No one knows you better than you do, so choose whatever makes you feel good, and add a little more of that to your life. Here are suggestions about how to feel renewed and refreshed while advocating for your loved one:

- **Review your Happiness L.I.S.T.:** If you haven't done anything on your L.I.S.T. lately, pull it out and add new items, or spend some time doing the ones that are already there.

- **Unplug and unwind:** Take time to unplug from your phone, laptop, and all social media today. When you reconnect later, you will see the world has managed to keep going without you, and you'll feel refreshed and ready to handle your next activity with a much more relaxed point of view.
- **Engage in physical contact:** Studies have shown that physical contact—from massage, sex, or hugs—reduces stress and releases a hormone called oxytocin, which boosts happiness.

Making time daily for self-care is an important habit to start while you're a caregiver and continue doing throughout your life.

Protect Yourself

In addition to the self-care items you just saw in the previous exercise, you want to do whatever you can to protect yourself from being hurt or overwhelmed by well-meaning friends, acquaintances, or even yourself. For example, if your loved one has been newly diagnosed with a disease, caring family members, friends, or work colleagues may offer their "I know someone who has that disease" stories—that you may not yet be ready to hear. It is okay to stop them by saying, "I truly appreciate your concern, but I simply can't listen to this story right now. I hope you understand." And then make contact again if and when you're ready to get their input.

Shield yourself from people in your life who are overly demanding of your time or emotions. If someone makes you feel unhappy or isn't willing to listen, stay away from that person as much as possible. This is difficult if he is a sibling and part of your family caregiving team, but do your best to minimize contact outside of the absolutely necessary caregiving discussions. Practice saying, "I'd like to have lunch with you, but I'm simply not in a position to be able to do that right now," so you can easily use it when needed.

You may also have to protect yourself from being on the receiving end of your care recipient's bad moods and emotional outbursts. You don't have control over how she speaks to you, but as a conscious caregiver, you absolutely can control how you respond to it.

If your care recipient is shouting at you, don't shout or even talk back. Become silent and wait until your care recipient is done. Then choose to either resume talking when she can continue in a normal speaking voice or leave politely.

CHAPTER SUMMARY

The following are takeaways, action steps, and reminders to help your caregiving journey progress smoothly.

- Being an advocate is made up of three parts: staying educated about your loved one's status, speaking up, and taking actions if he is unable. Follow these steps whether your loved one is aging in place, living in an assisted living community, or undergoing a hospitalization or rehabilitation stay in a skilled nursing facility.
- Create a medical health journal with *all* vital information about your loved one's health status. Be sure it is kept up-to-date so your family caregiving team and medical personnel can refer to it for correct information.
- There are numerous ways to communicate with doctors and their staff—patient portals, emails, texts, and phone. Ascertain their preferred way to connect, and follow up with them as needed. With your care recipient's permission, complete the required consent form(s) so the medical team can speak with you about your loved one's condition.
- Be sure to have your loved one complete and sign a durable power of attorney for health care or advance directive and keep it in the medical health journal. If your state offers the option of using a Physician's Orders for Life-Sustaining Treatment (POLST) form, have your loved one review it with the doctor, execute it, and keep it in the journal.
- As long as he is cognitively able, allow your loved one to direct her own medical care. Respect your loved one's right to do so, and be sure the medical staff does too. Consider changing doctors or other health providers if you find they aren't respectful of your care recipient's wishes.

- Make hospitalizations and rehabilitation stays better by connecting with medical staff in face-to-face interactions whenever possible. Let them understand you appreciate the hard work they're doing, but be your loved one's advocate by having efficient yet pleasant interactions whenever needed. Try not to upset your loved one if you have any complaints to pass along to the staff or if you're feeling stressed, worried, and overwhelmed.
- This is a critical time to practice self-care. Pamper yourself. Choose things to do that nourish your body, mind, or spirit. What activity have you done from your Happiness L.I.S.T. today? Get started now.

PART 3

The Progression of Conscious Caregiving

CHAPTER 7

Conscious Caregiving Options

Families come in different configurations today: traditional two-parent homes, one-parent households, or a combination of generations living under one roof. Similarly, caregiving living situations exist in various arrangements. Some care recipients will choose to "age in place" in their own homes rather than move to a senior care community, and some will want to move in with their caregivers.

In addition, more caregivers today find themselves part of the "sandwich generation," caring for aging parents while also raising their children. And some caregivers find themselves juggling the care needs for both parents simultaneously. In this chapter, you will learn to measure whether your care recipient is aging in place safely and if your home and family are equipped for another option—having a loved one move in with you. You'll also learn how to integrate caregiving with raising children, what to do if your adult children return home, and how to adjust your priorities when two care recipients need care at the same time.

CAREGIVING AT HOME

Some individuals and families feel strongly that they want to be the only ones caring for their loved ones and their care recipients should *not* move out of their own homes even as their care needs increase. Or, if they do move, it should be into a family member's home and not into an eldercare facility. Caregiving in home settings will be successful when you create a reliable family team and use conscious caregiving techniques for creative problem-solving and for self-care. If your loved one has memory loss, familiarity with his surroundings will help daily functioning and is another reason why you may want him to remain at home as long as possible.

If you plan to care for your loved one at home, here are some questions to ask yourself.

CONSCIOUS CONNECTIONS

Sometimes caregivers promise their loved ones that they will *never* move them out of their homes. While understandable, it's really not wise to lock yourself into this position, because no one knows what your loved one's future health needs will be. If she needs nursing care, you may not be equipped to be the primary caregiver and therefore may be unable to fulfill the promise you've made. Rather than promising you will never move your loved one, say, "I will care for you in your home [or mine] as long as it's possible."

Physical Environment

The first item to assess is whether your living environment has adequate space for your loved one to live with you safely and comfortably. Keep in mind that his care needs will probably increase over time, so analyze and plan space for now and in the future. Consider the following questions:

- ✓ Will your home allow your loved one to live there safely and comfortably?
- ✓ Are there any stairs your loved one will need to climb? Can ramps be built over them if he becomes wheelchair-bound? Can a stair lift be added to your staircase?

- ✓ Is there an extra bedroom and bathroom you can designate for your loved one? If not, who will she share these rooms with, and is that family member amenable to the change?
- ✓ Can the shower be entered easily, or is it a shower-tub combination that will require your loved one to climb in? Can it be renovated? Do grab bars need to be added in the shower and bathroom? Do the toilet seat and countertops need to be made higher?
- ✓ Does your home have senior-friendly flooring (i.e., no scatter rugs or uneven surfaces she could possibly trip on)? Do you have a garden path or patio also free of uneven surfaces and steps?
- ✓ Are the interior and exterior doorways wide enough to allow easy movement between rooms and outdoors if a wheelchair is used?
- ✓ Is there enough space for your family to still have ample privacy?
- ✓ Do you know what will happen to your loved one's current home after he moves out? Who will be responsible for its maintenance and carrying out the plan?

Once you know you have created or can create a safe and inviting space, turn your attention to the following less concrete questions.

Emotional Concerns

As a conscious caregiver, you've learned it's important to take the broadest view of any situation. Keep an open mind as you gather data and the input you need before analyzing and making decisions. Consider your loved one's potential social and emotional needs, as well as yours and your family's.

- ✓ If moving in with you is a big geographic change, will your loved one be leaving a circle of close friends? How easy will it be for her to connect with other older adults and have a source of new friendships? For example, is there a local senior center she can attend?
- ✓ What expectations do you, your immediate family, and your loved one have about living together? Consider the practical logistics (Can Mom stay home alone safely and for how long during the day or evening?), as well as less tangible aspects of having a new "roommate" (Dad thinks I'll always be available to chat whenever he wants me to.).
- ✓ Are you and your family ready and capable of taking care of your loved one at home? Are you willing to make the necessary changes and sacrifices in your work and personal life? Will everyone be agreeable to hiring professional caregivers to provide additional care if necessary?

You may not find these questions as easy to answer as the physical space questions, but nevertheless they should be explored.

Other Practical Considerations

Everyone, your care recipient included, needs to have clear expectations and a detailed picture of what the new living situation will look like. Think through carefully as many contingencies and "what ifs" as possible via the following questions:

- ✓ As the primary caregiver, how and when will you make time for daily self-care?
- ✓ Will your loved one need to find new health care providers?

- ✓ Will your loved one still be driving when she moves in with you? If not, is there reliable public transportation she can use, such as buses, trolleys, or trains? How available will family members be to give rides when needed? Would your care recipient feel comfortable using taxis, Uber, or Lyft to get around?
- ✓ If you are working, will you be able to decrease your hours or responsibilities when necessary to care for your loved one?
- ✓ Are there other local eldercare resources in your town or city that you and/or your loved one can utilize?
- ✓ What will the overall impact be on your *entire* family? Think about how it will affect everyone in the household, not just the primary caregiver, and others not living under your roof, such as siblings and anyone else on your family caregiving team.
- ✓ Can your family handle the additional financial costs of caregiving at home (e.g., increased food and utility bills)?
- ✓ If left home alone, would your loved one know what to do in case of an emergency and be able to take the appropriate safety actions without assistance? Does your family have an emergency plan and supplies ready?

So now that you know what questions to ask, let's take a look at caring for a loved one at home.

CASE STUDY: Elizabeth and Caregiving at Home

Gloria lived independently in her home until her late eighties. Her daughter-in-law, Elizabeth, slowly became her part-time caregiver, stopping by after work and on weekends to help Gloria when needed, as well as checking in by phone daily. As time went on it became more difficult for Gloria to live on her own, and Gloria finally agreed that she would like to come live with Elizabeth and Jay, Gloria's son.

Elizabeth says, "The experience of caring for my mother-in-law here in our home was so very rewarding. It's beneficial and such a wonderful experience for both us and Gloria."

Elizabeth knows they were fortunate to have living space on the ground floor, which permitted Gloria to live there without having to use any stairs. Gloria spent most of her time with them in the large family room or her "studio apartment" (the bedroom they redecorated for her). Jay modified Gloria's bathroom by converting the existing shower-tub combo into a shower only so she wouldn't have to climb over the side into a tub, and he also added grab bars and a shower chair.

When she first moved in, Gloria was well enough to stay alone during the days while Elizabeth and Jay worked full-time. A retired neighbor, Becky, volunteered to check on Gloria during the day if needed. Unfortunately, Gloria was diagnosed with ovarian cancer. Her granddaughter, Julianne, who was studying nursing, pitched in tremendously as Gloria's other caregiver during the summer while she was home from college, but by the time school began again for Julianne, Gloria's health had worsened. At that point the family hired a professional caregiver to care for Gloria until Elizabeth arrived home at 3:00 p.m. Elizabeth notes, "If you have a demanding job, you need to have a dynamite caregiver you can completely trust, or else you might consider taking a leave of absence from work. I cannot stress enough how wonderful it is to have an outside caregiver come in, if you can afford that." Both Elizabeth and Gloria interviewed the caregiver candidates, and Gloria herself chose the person she liked best.

Gloria, with the agreement of her family, decided not to proceed with the medical procedures her doctors suggested. "She just wanted to be comfortable at home," comments Elizabeth. Gloria passed away at ninety years old at home surrounded by family.

Elizabeth's perspective about the year Gloria lived with them: "We recommend this to anyone who has a family member, to do it if they possibly can."

CARING FOR TWO LOVED ONES SIMULTANEOUSLY

Your parents will probably pass away at different times, one at a significantly or somewhat younger age than the other. In this case, you will have only one loved one to focus all of your caregiving efforts on. But what happens if both of your parents live long lives and then start declining at the same time in different ways (physically or cognitively)? Or if one remains relatively healthy while the other declines rapidly? Or if they "take turns" in their decline? If you're married, you might need to help out your aging and declining in-laws too. How can you cope best under these changing circumstances?

For a conscious caregiver, navigating these various life situations is complex. You strive to do your best to meet multiple people's needs while still preserving time for daily self-care. Let's take a look at the ins and outs of providing assistance for two care recipients at the same time.

Prioritize Their Needs

You will have to prioritize the needs of each of your loved ones to determine whom you should spend more time with on a daily or weekly basis. You may need to accompany one to pressing doctors' appointments and do the resulting follow-up steps, such as taking her for lab tests or filling prescriptions. The other parent may want you to go with her to a much-anticipated social function. Or, in more extreme circumstances, each could be hospitalized at the same time, possibly even in different hospitals, and you'll find yourself shuttling between two locations.

CONSCIOUS CONNECTIONS

Hopefully your parents will already understand the intricacies and constraints involved in your double caregiving duties and won't put additional pressure on you. But if they do, listen mindfully to what they're saying (or possibly complaining about) and then share your caregiving to-do list with them. Explain the order you've decided upon for the items and your reasons why. Ask them if they have suggestions to improve the plan and/or get things done more efficiently. Seeing your list in writing should open their eyes to all of the pressing items you need to get done. If you enlist their aid, they might find ways to make things easier on you ("There's no rush for that, so take it off the list."), or they may at least back down from making more demands on you or the team.

All of these scenarios can happen with care recipient couples, so plan ahead. Caring for two parents or other aging loved ones simultaneously takes an even higher level of organization, planning, and decision-making than when caring for one person. Ask your family caregiving team and/or your personal support team (such as your spouse or teenage or college-aged children) for help in covering the differing responses needed, as well as in planning for the "what ifs" that may come up.

If you're struggling to prioritize, first, use the mindfulness process to determine the priorities of their joint care needs. Carefully think through the broad picture of everything to be done for both. Then utilize the process/exercise for making a to-do list given in Chapter 3, writing down everything you must and want to do for them, both short and long term. Indicate the amount of time each task should take and who on the family team can best accomplish that task. Prioritize your list beginning with the top three items, and that includes delegating things to appropriate team members.

Separating Spouses

In some care situations, you may need to go as far as separating spouses, either short or long term, due to the different levels of care needed. This is a heart-wrenching experience, for both you and your loved ones. And it may make your life more difficult, too, as you must then make time to give care to two people in separate locations.

If you want both parents to continue living high-quality lives, speaking about this option is a must. Follow the same guidelines given in Chapter 4 for communicating about hard issues. It will be a highly emotional decision to make and will take time to accept. After the decision is made, the healthier parent may find relief from the anxiety he had been feeling in this difficult situation, even though the solution itself can be agonizing. For long-married couples, this huge change is often filled with guilt and embarrassment, but a choice like this stems from deep love and caring. It's hard to explain this unusual and unwanted separation to extended family and others, but do your best to assuage any worries they may have. Also reassure the healthier parent that by moving his spouse to a more appropriate level of care (which also allows more time for self-care), he is being an even better caregiver.

CASE STUDY: Linda and Separating Loved Ones

One of the biggest regrets of my caregiving years happened during the time my parents lived separately. When they were both in their nineties my mom declined cognitively due to Alzheimer's disease, while my dad continued being sharp mentally. But at age ninety-five he fell and broke his hip and subsequently underwent hip-replacement surgery. Fortunately, he made a full recovery and even returned to league bowling on his bowling team.

After living in an assisted living community for about two years, my parents both moved to a six-bed residential care facility. At the time, the doctor suggested they live apart, in two different houses owned by the same company, because my mom's care needs were much greater than my dad's. It seemed like the way to provide the best environment for both, and after my dad and I discussed it and toured several, the decision was made to move. He lived in a home with other, more alert seniors he could engage with, while my mom received the necessary, more intense memory care. The houses were located only a few minutes away from one another, so I would pick up my dad a few times a week and we'd drive over to visit my mom together.

What I didn't do was make time to have fun visits with my dad alone. I assumed visiting his wife of more than seventy years would be what he longed to do, and yes, I'm sure he wanted to visit her. But I didn't think to ask if he would he like to take a scenic drive or go to a movie with me instead. We were both focused on my mom because she had a "diagnosis." If I could do something over, it would be to make time for quality one-on-one visits with him during that period of time, which turned out to be the last years of his life. It remains a huge caregiving regret. However, I was fortunate to have a wonderful cousin who also lived near them. Not only did she and her husband visit my mom and dad, but she also took my dad out for ice cream and other pleasant outings, for which I will be grateful always.

CONSCIOUS CONNECTIONS

According to *Caregiving in the U.S. 2015*, 84 percent of family caregivers stated that they could use more information about or help with caregiving topics. And the majority also reported that conversations about the need for self-care are *not* taking place with their health care providers. As a conscious caregiver, you can become part of the solution by sharing these statistics and asking for needed information, seeking assistance, and holding meaningful conversations with medical practitioners during or after your caregiving journey.

Double-Duty Self-Care

Caring for two loved ones simultaneously is stressful and can lead to caregiver burnout. Fortunately, when you feel like you don't have even one free moment to focus on yourself while caring for two people, there is a simple technique you can do to alleviate stress and avoid burnout: create positive affirmations (short, powerful statements) that you think silently to yourself or say out loud to consciously change your reality. This can be done in the midst of all caregiving activities and should become an integral part of your customized self-care toolkit.

EXERCISE: Create Positive Affirmations

Your thoughts can either uplift you or tear you down. Negative thinking hurts and wears you out emotionally, often for no legitimate reason. Use mindfulness to stop, become aware of your brain chatter, and "hear" yourself think. What *are* your inner thoughts? Are you putting yourself down by thinking or saying, "No matter what I do, it's never enough" or "I can't believe how stupid what I did was"?

Instead of slathering love and care on only your care recipients, shower yourself with a dose of that love and TLC by replacing negative thoughts and words with positive affirmations in order to lower your anxiety level and reduce tension. For example, think or say aloud sayings such as:

- "I always do my best to care for my loved one."
- "I stay calm and relaxed in all situations."
- "I trust myself to make the right decisions."
- "I love myself; therefore, if I make a mistake I forgive myself."
- "I love myself; therefore, I make time to do an activity from my Happiness L.I.S.T."

Or you can create your own meaningful affirmations that resonate with your personality and caregiving situation. Use words you're comfortable with and ones that create happy feelings inside. Repeat one to three of them at a time, giving your brain time to imprint the connection between the kinder words you're speaking to yourself and the good feelings that result. Saying positive affirmations daily will become a pleasing habit you can do anytime and anywhere.

CONSCIOUS CAREGIVING WITH KIDS AT HOME

When my parents moved cross-country into an assisted living community in my hometown, my son was eleven years old. Today, more men and women in their forties through sixties are finding themselves in a similar situation. We are part of the sandwich generation, meaning we are caring for at least one aging parent and raising children at the same time. As such, you face unique caregiving challenges (responding to the needs of family members of vastly different ages, from children to older adults) and competing demands (should I attend my teenage daughter's annual violin recital or stay with Dad during his MRI?) and may feel pulled in multiple directions every day in terms of time, energy, and priorities.

Conscious caregiving will help you survive this hectic period in your life. Pause and assess the practical parts of intergenerational living, acknowledging both the positives and negatives. For example, everyone benefits by beng exposed to relatives with a wide range of interests and hobbies to share. On the other hand, each person may have to give up some degree of privacy at times or find they crave some time alone in their own home. Think through ways to accentuate the positives and use creative problem-solving on the harder challenges. Put the time management ideas in Chapter 3 to use, and realize that you may need to reprioritize your to-do lists even more frequently.

Also, just as you have periodic family meetings with your adult siblings, hold nuclear family meetings weekly with everyone present. This way, your immediate family will understand that this is a family project to work on together harmoniously. Sit down to map out the tasks that need to get done, figure out the most efficient ways to do them, and ask for volunteers or assign age-appropriate jobs so you're not stressed-out trying to do everything yourself. As you'll read in the following sections, your parents and even the youngest children can contribute to the effort in meaningful ways. Keep in mind that one day your children and your parent(s) will no longer be living under your roof, so appreciate this precious time together and create joyful experiences too.

"Being deeply loved by someone gives you strength, while loving someone deeply gives you courage."

—Lao Tzu, Chinese philosopher

Caregiving with Younger Kids

Whether your children are preschoolers, elementary school–age, or teenagers, they should belong to your caregiving team. The intergenerational connections formed when living together adds depth to the whole family's life that other people don't have the opportunity to experience. Be alert for and capitalize on the teachable moments that present themselves regarding love, sacrifice, and compassion. Children in preschool and kindergarten today are extremely tech-savvy and will be happy to help your parents use the TV remote control, tablet, smartphone, or computer. They can also play games, walk the dog, or share hobbies together, giving you a break for a few minutes to do other tasks or practice self-care. In fact, you may find an enjoyable activity on your

Happiness L.I.S.T. you can all do together. Creating fun family memories while doing self-care is the ultimate victory!

In addition, depending upon their health status, your aging parents can help in a variety of ways. If they're still driving, they can take your children to school, to after-school activities, and to friends' houses for playdates and birthday parties. Or perhaps your loved one is able to help with daily light housekeeping tasks, such as loading the dishwasher, watering the plants, clipping coupons, or folding towels. Every chore that gets done is one less for you to do. The oldest generation is also a resource for sage advice on many subjects, for both your children and you. Be open to hearing the wisdom they want to share.

CONSCIOUS CONNECTIONS

According to a 2013 study done by the Pew Research Center, "Nearly half (47 percent) of adults in their 40s and 50s have a parent age 65 or older and are either raising a young child or financially supporting a grown child (age 18 or older)."

Caregiving with Adult Children

Adult children who move back in with their parents are called "boomerangs" and should definitely be integrated into the family caregiving team. While they may be away at work or school during the day, at nights and on weekends they should be *expected* to participate in both caregiving and household responsibilities. For example, they can be in charge of managing your loved one's medications (making sure they are taken properly and refilled as needed), run errands with or for their grandparents, and spend time sharing hobbies with them too. They will reap the same benefits of living with the older generation that younger children do, and may appreciate even more the special bond they create with their grandparents. Additionally, adult children might be able to contribute financially to care costs depending upon their income.

CHAPTER SUMMARY

The following are takeaways, action steps, and reminders to help your caregiving journey progress smoothly.

- Before your care recipient moves in (or you move in with her) consider every angle. How will it affect you and your whole caregiving team? Examine the physical environment, expectations for day-to-day life, emotional concerns, and practical considerations.
- There are several ways to make living together easier after many years apart. Keep a sense of humor. Know and enforce your boundaries of space, time, and willingness to do what it takes to make this living arrangement successful.
- Hire paid caregivers and bring in hospice service for additional layers of care and to permit you to arrange time away from the house while knowing your loved one is safe and well cared for.
- When caring for two people, it becomes more complex to meet each one's various needs and not lose yourself in the shuffle. Planning ahead sooner and enlisting the help of others on your caregiving team are important. Continue to assess your loved ones' needs and adjust their individual care plans accordingly. Don't treat two individuals as one unit requiring the same care.
- If you have to separate your loved ones, do your utmost not to feel guilty. Remember that their needs are different, and you are making the best decision for each of them that you can under these circumstances. Arrange for them to visit each other as much as they'd like.
- Use positive affirmations daily to stop the negative brain chatter, lower anxiety, reduce stress, and avoid burnout. Create statements you're comfortable saying in your own words, and practice them until they become an ingrained habit to be used in any caregiving situation.

- If an aging loved one moves in with you, your children (at any age) can be assets on the family caregiving team. Intergenerational living has its pros and cons, but by practicing conscious caregiving, the good should outweigh the bad and everyone will benefit. Increase your organizational practices, continuously remain flexible, and keep reprioritizing everyone's needs.
- Adult children who move back home can take on larger responsibilities than their younger siblings. Nuclear family meetings should be held weekly so the caregiving and household responsibilities are shared and don't rest solely on your shoulders.

CHAPTER 8

What to Expect When Making the Transition to Assisted Living

Few aging parents or spouses want their family members to give up their own lives in order to care for them. When your loved ones are no longer safe living in their homes, or if providing care for them is interfering greatly with your everyday life and health, another option is moving them into an assisted living community where they can live independently and get assistance as their care needs increase. How to determine when it's time and how to find the best place for your loved ones to live are discussed here, along with information on downsizing, how-tos for the overall move, and specific moving-day suggestions. You'll also learn how to combat negative self-talk, guilt, or sadness that results from the move. Finally, we'll discuss how your caregiving role doesn't end; it just morphs into a new operating mode.

WHAT IS ASSISTED LIVING?

Assisted living combines independence with personalized care for your loved one in a residential setting. There isn't one "look" to an assisted living community; each one is unique. Settings vary from a high-rise apartment building in a city to a group of low-rise buildings with cottage-like architecture surrounded by acres of grounds. Living quarters could be a studio apartment, a one-bedroom apartment, or a shared two-bedroom apartment for a married couple or unrelated single roommates. Meals are served daily in a common dining room for all residents.

Assisted living is for older adults who are social and active but may also need some level of help with daily activities, such as, but not limited to, meal preparation, medication management, transportation, laundry, bathing, and dressing. Some residents may have memory loss or need assistance with mobility, incontinence, or other physical challenges.

Most communities also offer housekeeping services, transportation to local shopping areas and doctors' appointments, twenty-four-hour security, exercise and wellness programs, and a full calendar of recreational activities covering many hobbies and interests.

Costs depend upon the community's location, size of living quarters, and services used by the residents. Most charge month-to-month rates as in a standard rental apartment agreement, with additional fees for extra care services. Some offer only a longer-term, "buy-in" agreement which is designed more like a home purchase where you pay a substantial, one-time, entrance charge plus monthly fees for services. Residents or their families pay from their own personal financial resources for assisted living.

HOW TO KNOW WHEN IT'S TIME TO MOVE

Older adults decline in different ways—physically, cognitively, or both—and at various speeds. Because every caregiving situation is unique, there isn't one simple answer to the question, "How do I know when it's time to move my loved one from his or her home to assisted living?" That said, the most critical question to ask is, "Is my loved one safe living at home alone?" This question must be applied to his or her physical safety, cognitive functioning, and emotional state.

EXERCISE: Your Loved One's Safety Questionnaire

If you're wondering if it's time to move your loved one into assisted living, answer the following questions before making a decision on whether or not to act:

Physical Safety

- Would your loved one know what to do in case of an emergency? Would she be capable of taking those actions?
- Is he a continuing fall risk? Have there been a series of falls at home?
- Has your loved one been to the ER several times over a short period for "minor" reasons, such as dehydration?
- Has there been any unusual weight loss or gain?
- Are your loved one's hearing and vision abilities the same? Do you notice him keeping the TV volume extra loud or sitting closer than normal to the screen?
- Is your loved one moving as well as before? Is her gait regular? Does she seem weak or off-balance when walking, getting up from a chair, or rising from bed? Is she holding onto furniture or walls when moving around at home?
- Is your loved one able to manage stairs safely?
- Does he seem less energetic?
- Have your loved one's sleep habits changed? Is she sleeping more or less than in previous years?
- Does he have bruises or scratches anywhere, or swollen legs, ankles, or feet?
- Does your loved one need help dressing, bathing, or using the toilet? Are her hair, finger- and toenails, and teeth (or dentures) properly maintained?

- Is your loved one taking medications (both prescribed and over-the-counter) as directed? Is he clear on what the medications are for and what the required dosages are? Is he keeping up with refills as needed? Are there expired medications in the medicine cabinet?
- Is your loved one going for regular doctors' appointments, including visits to the primary care physician, any specialists, the optometrist, and the dentist?
- Is your loved one using her glasses, hearing aids, and mobility tools (cane, walker, wheelchair, scooter, etc.)? Are these assistance devices well maintained?
- If your loved one needs to administer injections or do wound care, is he able to do so properly and refill supplies as needed?

Measuring Vulnerability

Seniors who live alone might crave companionship, which makes them easy prey for those who want to take advantage of their loneliness and vulnerability. Consider the following:

- Is your loved one a potential target of scammers?
- Would he give out personal information on the telephone to a stranger? Can your loved one hear well enough on the phone to identify the speaker quickly?
- Would your loved one open the front door to strangers or solicitors?
- Is she comfortably in control of finances and doing banking successfully, either online or in person? Are the bills being paid on time? Have there been any irregularities with credit cards, debit cards, or bank accounts?

- If your loved one is using a computer or tablet, is he savvy enough to recognize and avoid online schemes and scammers?

Psychological Safety

- Does your loved one seem like the person you remember, or does something seem different or "off"? Trust your instincts.
- Is he repeating stories or questions? Is he more forgetful or showing signs of confusion?
- Does your loved one seem depressed or anxious? Is she crying or getting angry more easily? Is she fearful of things that didn't cause worry before?
- Has your loved one lost interest in activities and/or hobbies she used to enjoy? Is she staying home more and limiting social engagements?
- Do you see any signs of new or increased alcohol or drug use?

Environmental Safety

- How is your loved one's driving? Do his reflexes seem slower? Is any loss of mobility having an impact on his driving? Has your loved one gotten lost going to familiar places? Has he stopped driving at night or longer distances?
- Are there new dents or dings in the car or garage? Can your loved one explain how they happened?
- Does the house look and smell clean? Is "deep cleaning" being done to the house?
- Are the linens fresh? Is your loved one able to do laundry, or is it piling up?

- Is the yard neat and well groomed?
- Are pets and/or houseplants being taken care of appropriately?
- Are the refrigerator, pantry, countertops, and cupboards clean?
- Is the food old or expired? Check dates on milk, cottage cheese, and other perishables.
- Is your loved one still cooking and/or using food delivery services in order to maintain a healthy diet?
- Can she safely use appliances (e.g., stove, microwave, iron)?
- Has food that should be refrigerated been left out on the counter? Are other kitchen items placed where they should be?
- Is the house cluttered? Are garbage and trash accumulating?
- Is the mail in unopened piles? Are newspapers being read and discarded in a timely manner?

After you answer these questions, share, evaluate, and discuss the input collected by each member of your caregiving team at a family meeting. Your loved one may be declining or not coping with daily living as well as before, but don't rush into decisions that she may not need or welcome. You may decide what's needed first is to keep a vigilant eye on your loved one to see if the changes are temporary or increasing. Some things could be corrected easily through adjustments in her home. Or you may decide it's time to discuss other options, such as getting in-home care or moving to an assisted living community. Exactly when it's time to move will depend upon your loved one's condition, her current home environment, and the safety analysis your team does.

CONSCIOUS CONNECTIONS

Moving your loved one from a long-established home will take a series of conversations over time. Use mindful speaking to impart the message that you want what's best for him. Use mindful listening to better understand your loved one's questions, feelings, and degree of acceptance of the idea to move. Read more about mindful communication in Chapter 4.

FIND THE BEST FACILITY FOR YOUR LOVED ONE

Even before the decision is made that your care recipient will move, begin collecting names and going on tours of assisted living communities. Your initial list could possibly have between five to ten communities on it, which may be too overwhelming for an older adult to sift through. It's best for you to do the initial whittling down of the choices, through online research and reviews, talking to friends who have or had family living there, and/or initial visits to the communities. There are many facets of community living to take in and assess in order to find the right fit for your loved one.

Touring Tips

To save time and avoid wearing out your loved one, do the initial tours on your own and narrow down the list of acceptable communities to no more than three for your loved one to see. You know your care recipient best, so listen to your intellect and your intuition while touring different communities. Don't let a beautiful interior distract you from investigating the quality of care. Yes, your loved one may be happy because the lobby and common areas are pleasing to the eye and the new apartment has a scenic view, but you need to go beyond the surface glitz to ensure the facility can meet your loved one's current and future care needs. Visit the facility more than once, on different days and times, to get a comprehensive picture of what life there is really like.

EXERCISE: Use the Facility Evaluation Checklist

If you're not sure what questions to ask or what to look for in an assisted living facility, use the following checklist. Make separate copies of this list to take on tours of each facility. Write notes, including both the facts and your impressions during and/or immediately after each tour while they're fresh in your mind. Use it as a springboard for additional questions, ideas, preferences, and priorities for everyone involved in making the decision to consider.

Overall Questions after a Tour

- ✓ Is the facility affordable?
- ✓ Is it convenient for most family members to visit? Most importantly, is it close to the primary caregiver's home?
- ✓ Is it in close proximity to your loved one's doctors and medical services?
- ✓ Do the facility's care programs meet your loved one's needs? Will they be able to continue providing quality care in the future when decline happens?
- ✓ Do the current residents appear content and well groomed?
- ✓ Does the setting seem calm, comfortable, and home-like?
- ✓ Can you picture your loved one living there happily, after the initial transition is made?

Staffing

✓ What is the ratio of staff to residents—overall and also broken down by job category (e.g., caregivers, nurses, food service)?

✓ What are the licenses for the nursing staff? (How many RNs, LPNs or LVNs, CNAs, etc.?)

✓ Is there an RN working on the premises or at least on call 24/7?

✓ Who supervises the caregivers, and how is the supervision done?

✓ What type of background checks are the potential caregivers subject to? Ask which company or service does the checks, and request to see a recent one. Based on their reply, you may have to "go with your gut" about this. Facilities may be unable to share background checks with you legally due to labor privacy laws. Rely on your instincts if necessary.

✓ How long is the instruction for new caregivers? How and by whom is the training done (e.g., classrooms, online, on-the-job)? How much continuing education is required for veteran caregivers? When is this continuing education offered, and do the staff have allotted time to participate?

✓ How many of the staff are trained specifically in your loved one's diagnosis (e.g. colostomy care, dementia care)?

✓ What is the turnover rate among caregivers at the facility? What has it been over the past several years compared to the present year?

✓ How long have the majority of current employees been working there? (Low turnover means the facility is doing something right.)

✓ Do the staff greet the residents by name and really seem to know and care about their welfare?

- ✓ What medical staffing (physicians, PT, OT, lab work, x-rays, etc.) is provided in the facility? If hired from an outside provider, is there a regular schedule for visits, and how often do they come?
- ✓ What happens if your loved one needs more care, either immediately or long term? What actual medical care can be done on the premises based on state licensing regulations?
- ✓ Are families allowed to hire health care workers for one-on-one care in addition to the existing staff? What screening and steps are required to put someone in place?
- ✓ Does the state require facilities to obtain a hospice waiver? (This is an authorization to allow your loved one to live there with hospice care until the end of his or her life.)

Meals

- ✓ Can you and your loved one eat a meal in their dining room and see the menus for all other meals? (This is not an unusual request.)
- ✓ How many meals are served per day or week? Are snacks readily available in between meals? Does the menu look nutritious?
- ✓ Are special dietary needs accommodated and how easily?
- ✓ Is the dining room clean with a pleasant atmosphere that encourages conversation and eating? Or does it seem noisy and/or hectic?
- ✓ How do the staff monitor the residents' nutritional intake? How will they know if your loved one misses a meal, and what happens if so?
- ✓ Do the staff help residents based on their abilities (e.g., cutting up food, helping them carry plates if a meal is served buffet style, pureeing food)?

- ✓ Is there tray service allowed if your care recipient doesn't feel well enough to go to the dining room for meals? Is there an additional charge for that service?
- ✓ Can family and/or friends eat in the dining room with the residents, and is there a charge for these guest meals?

Programs and Services

- ✓ Is medication administered and by which staff members? Are refills ordered by the facility, or is the family required to bring them? If possible, see where medications are kept when not being dispensed. Most state laws require that they be stored in a locked room, cabinet, or closet.
- ✓ Is transportation (bus, van, and/or car service) available for local medical appointments and shopping? Is there an additional charge beyond a certain mileage radius?
- ✓ Is there a full- or part-time activities director? Ask for a sample activities calendar for the week or month.
- ✓ Observe what activities are going on while you tour. What are the residents' attendance and participation levels at the activities? Are caregivers participating in activities with the residents, or do they look disinterested or unengaged?
- ✓ Are the scheduled activities ones your care recipient will enjoy? Do they match his interests and hobbies? If not, does the activities director seem amenable to adding a different activity your loved one enjoys?
- ✓ Are trips to local special events and/or scenic drives offered throughout the year?
- ✓ How are birthdays, anniversaries, and other special occasions celebrated there?

- ✓ Can you picture your loved one "fitting in" and becoming friends with the residents you see?

Environment

- ✓ How clean, bright, and airy is the apartment or studio your loved one will live in?
- ✓ Are the units furnished, or will you need to provide furniture? Is there enough room to bring whatever items you will need to make it feel like home?
- ✓ Are the indoor public areas and outdoor areas secured, well lit, and safe? What are the components of their security system? Cameras, staff, and/or alarms? Have there been any unsavory incidents there?
- ✓ Are all indoor spaces easy to navigate, handicap-accessible, and safety-oriented? For example, are there hand railings along corridors? Chairs to rest in while waiting for an elevator or walking down a long hallway?
- ✓ Does the overall environment promote independence yet keep safety at the forefront?
- ✓ Is there an emergency button or cord in the apartment bathroom? Is there one elsewhere, such as in the bedroom?
- ✓ How well equipped is the facility to handle a natural disaster, such as a hurricane, tornado, or earthquake? Ask to read their emergency plan and see their stored emergency supplies. What training do the staff get in emergency preparedness? Where would residents be evacuated to if need be?
- ✓ Is there adequate parking for residents and visitors? If there is assigned resident parking, ask to see where your loved one's space will be.

Family Involvement

✓ How often are care plan meetings held to address your loved one's needs?

✓ Do the staff offer an "open-door policy" for family meetings, suggestions, and concerns?

✓ How do the staff inform family members about changes in their loved one's condition and/or changing care needs?

✓ How do they communicate with families if an emergency occurs, either personal in nature or a natural disaster?

✓ Are there set visiting hours? Can visitors use the amenities and participate in events or outings with loved ones?

✓ What is the procedure for taking your loved one out for a day, weekend, or extended vacation?

✓ Are family education workshops and/or support groups offered at the facility for residents' family members?

After gathering information about each community, analyze your notes with your loved one's needs in mind. Which one will offer the best care overall while keeping her as active and socially engaged as is comfortable?

Do Your Due Diligence

After you take a tour, ask to speak with several residents and their family members to get feedback about their experiences there. See if what they share meshes with what the staff said about what it's like to live there. Yes, the staff will probably only give you contact information for their "satisfied customers," but at least you are getting other people's perspectives. Listen carefully to their stories and comments.

Some older adults will be unsure if they're ready to move into assisted living. Ask the management if your loved one might try a short-term stay to experience life there and make a more educated decision. Of course, this could work for or against your preferred outcome, so you may want to skip this if you've decided your loved one is no longer safe living alone in his or her home and must move.

Assisted living communities are regulated or certified in all fifty states and are inspected by the state's regulatory agency. Ask for the most recent state inspection survey results and note the following:

- The date of the report to ascertain it is current data.
- If citations were given for a particular service area, ask detailed questions about it and what they have done or are doing to correct it.
- Compare the number of deficiencies cited to the state average. Be wary of any community with a high number of deficiencies compared with other facilities in the local area and the state average.
- Check their Better Business Bureau rating as another assessment resource. An "A+" rating is not a guarantee, but it is an indication of a business's reliability and performance.

Keep in mind that, although this is a care industry, most assisted living communities are for-profit businesses.

MAKING MOVING DAY EASIER FOR EVERYONE

Moving from one home to another is difficult and stressful at any age, but moving from one's home of many years can be even more so, due to both the number of belongings accumulated over a lifetime and their sentimental value. As with many other aspects of caregiving, preplanning and organization are the keys to making the actual move easier.

Using a conscious caregiver's approach, think in advance about the move in general and also zoom in on details for moving day. This will help both you and your loved one stay as relaxed and comfortable as possible. Yes, glitches may occur on moving day, but they should be at a minimum with a carefully thought-out plan (and alternate plans B and C if necessary).

> "Start by doing what's necessary; then do what's possible; and suddenly you are doing the impossible."
>
> —Francis of Assisi, Italian saint

Discuss Logistics Ahead of Time

This is a perfect time to hold another family team meeting to discuss moving logistics: One person can research and hire a moving company or be responsible for securing a pickup or other truck for use on moving day. Another person can be the liaison with the assisted living community staff. The primary caregiver or whoever will be visiting most often is the best choice for this role. Another might be in charge of gathering and packing home decor accessories, personal toiletries, and clothing to be moved. One more can be in charge of finding out about cable TV and/or Internet hookups in the apartment and moving any computers or TVs safely. Another can be in charge of changing banks if needed and sending out change-of-address notifications to people and services that need to know about your loved one's move. It will be a lot easier for everyone if the tasks are shared among the caregiving team members.

Downsize

Sorting to downsize takes time, so it's never too early to start the process. Begin to tackle the larger areas first, such as the basement, garage, closets, and attic. Do it in small chunks of time so as not to become overwhelmed with the enormity of moving an entire household. Set a timer for one hour every day to devote to this project. It will feel much better to accomplish a little bit each day than to devote a full day (or days) and be tired out by lunchtime.

As long as your loved one is able, include her in decisions and tasks, such as deciding which clothes to take. Let your loved one choose a friend or charity to donate unwanted clothing to. Listen to your loved one's preferences about what to keep and why these items are important. For example, my father was a champion bridge player who won many trophies of all sizes and shapes over his lifetime. While he didn't have room for all of them when my parents downsized, it was important for him to select several prized, sterling silver trophies to display in their new home.

To choose what to part with and what to keep, walk through your loved one's current home with her and use green, red, and yellow Post-it notes, labels, or tape as markers. Items that must be moved are given a green label. Those that should be given away or put in storage are labeled red. Things with yellow labels are to be reconsidered once the essential items are decided upon.

Consider not moving multiples of items (such as coats or mugs), large pieces of furniture, rarely worn jewelry, throw rugs that may cause someone to trip, and seldom-used items. Also consider renting a storage unit for several months if your loved one is not quite ready to part with certain items that have sentimental value or should be saved for posterity. It won't hurt to store furniture and other mementos for up to a year, giving your loved one a chance to reevaluate the value of these items later.

Figure Out the Physical Space

When you've selected the exact apartment in the assisted living community your loved one is moving into, take a tape measure and record the physical space available. Do your best to make at least a rough sketch of the floor plan. This will give your family the data needed to figure out which larger furniture items will fit and decide on their new locations and how they'll be moved.

The assisted living community is normally responsible for deep cleaning, repainting, and recarpeting the apartment as needed, as well as doing all necessary repairs before move-in day. Meet in advance with the staff member in charge of getting the apartment in tip-top shape and follow up in a nice, not pesky, way to be sure everything is finished before moving day.

If possible, get the apartment decorated and set up for your loved one (except for clothing, medications, and personal toiletries) before moving day. Communities are usually agreeable to and even encourage this. It's ideal if you can keep your care recipient away from the chaos of unpacking. Plus, it's really nice for your loved one to walk in and see family photos hung on the walls and his favorite easy chair waiting in the living room.

Pack a Special Suitcase

Help your loved one pack a special suitcase for moving day itself. It should include clothing, toiletries, medications, glasses, hearing aids, and important papers. If the community or moving company expects payment that day, be sure you are prepared with the correct amount and form of payment. Some moving companies require cash payment. It's good to also have on hand some favorite snacks and drinks with paper plates and plastic utensils. If the apartment isn't completely decorated, you may want to bring a hammer, nails, other basic tools, and some cleaning supplies, such as paper towels, spray cleaner, and soap, just in case. However, finishing touches to the decor can be made over time. Perhaps your loved one would like to live there for a few days or even weeks before deciding where to place the artwork in her new home.

AFTER PLACEMENT

Although you know you made the best decision you could in moving your loved one to an assisted living community, you and other family caregiving team members may still feel worry, guilt, anxiety, and sadness over it. You feel relief because your loved one is safe and cared for, but these other emotions are also real.

Moving is a large adjustment for both you and your loved one. Your established caregiving routine and amount of time spent together will probably change. Be patient with yourself and your loved one. It will take time for all of you to make the transition to daily life in this new community. Acknowledge that it's a new stage of life for all of you. You may feel sadness because it means your loved one's disease is progressing and he is declining. Especially in the case of a spouse, you may also feel depressed because you can no longer provide all of the care he needs. You may have promised you would never move your spouse out of your home. Who ever thought you would have to live apart? Sessions with a therapist or clergy member are often beneficial for a family caregiver and care recipient during this transition time.

CONSCIOUS CONNECTIONS

Be aware of any of your own negative self-talk. Don't think or use statements such as, "I put her away." If you catch yourself doing this, write down your guilty, angry, or negative statement. Then ask yourself if it's accurate and reasonable. Does it express the reality of the situation? If not, rewrite the statement using more positive words. For example, instead of writing, "I put her away," use this sentence: "I placed Mom in assisted living so she can continue to enjoy life in a safer environment."

This is another crucial time in your caregiving journey to be vigilant about practicing self-care. Some of the time previously spent caring for your loved one is now freed up, so remember to spend time doing activities that will relax and restore you. Ironically, acknowledging that you have more time for self-care after placement may lead to more feelings of guilt, creating a vicious cycle. Instead of feeling guilty, focus on finding your "good." Refer back to the Happiness L.I.S.T. and select some activities to do. Give yourself permission to have fun—you deserve it. Embracing an enjoyable activity, such as taking a bubble bath, spending time with friends, doing yoga, singing, or reading, will help dispel the worries rattling around in your head.

Caregiving Doesn't End after a Move

If you're worried that your caregiving role will end once your loved one moves to an assisted living facility, don't be! You will still be an integral part of your loved one's care, but in a somewhat different role. While you won't have to do the heavy physical care any longer, there will be other responsibilities. Based on the level of care you've arranged for, you may need to do your loved one's laundry and/or medication management, for example. Depending upon his level of independence at the time of the move, you may decide to have the post office forward his mail to your home and bring it to open together when you visit. Or you may begin to handle your loved one's health insurance benefits and claims, making sure all medical care invoices and insurance company correspondence are correct. This often is a good time to become more knowledgeable about his or her financial assets and status.

As much as you may be looking forward to not having to be the hands-on caregiver after placement, you may find it hard to give up the reins of care to the professional assisted living staff. If you're struggling with this, use mindfulness tools to help you pause and become conscious of your feelings about having to share your primary caregiving job with professionals. Try saying some positive affirmations to ease the transition and decrease negative feelings. For example, you may say something like: "It feels strange not to help Dad with everything like before, but I know the caregivers here will always do their best for him." Give yourself a month minimum to allow sufficient time to come to terms with this shift in your caregiving role and to see how your loved one is adjusting. Chances are it will work out well for everyone involved. But if you, your loved one, or other team members aren't satisfied, meet with the appropriate assisted living staff to discuss possible solutions for any issues. Most communities will go above and beyond to keep residents and their families pleased. If changes are implemented and improvement isn't seen, it may be time for a family meeting to discuss moving your loved one to another community.

CASE STUDY: Patti and the Assisted Living Transition

Patti, age seventy, describes the transition she went through after moving her mom, Jane, age ninety, into assisted living:

"The community was only a mile and a half away from our home, so it was almost like she was living with us. It was hard for me to let go and hand it over to the professionals. They suggested we back off for a week so they could help her get to know the staff and routine there. I was totally in favor of that, and was able to do it. Breaking those kinds of ties made sense to me so they could be in charge of her care. But it was tough, living that close and knowing we could even walk over there. In the beginning, I was there a lot after the first week, even three or four times a week, because I wanted to know what kind of care she was getting. I had my antennae up every time I went there, got to know who did what, and it was all good. I did it in a way that I didn't get in the way of any of the workers. One challenging thing was learning how to voice my opinion but without getting on the staff's bad side."

Patti explains more about how her role changed over time: "Initially I did ask a lot of questions for a lot of different reasons, not only for my mom's benefit but because I wanted the knowledge too. I eventually had to let go of some of that. When you have too many fish in the pot, somebody has to be in charge and it wasn't necessarily me anymore. I wanted them to know I was an interested party, but I didn't *have* to make the final decision every time. I was eventually happy to take the back seat because the staff knew what they were doing with her disease (dementia). Yet in some ways I felt like I was more involved, just in a different way."

Patti went through several stages of letting go of her mom's care. It may be a difficult adjustment, but it can be done.

CHAPTER SUMMARY

The following are takeaways, action steps, and reminders to help your caregiving journey progress smoothly.

- When deciding if your loved one should move, ask yourself, "Is she safe living at home alone?" Other areas to check into are your loved one's physical and emotional states, personal hygiene, and daily functioning at home.
- There are many aspects to consider when researching and touring assisted living facilities. Don't get distracted by a pretty environment; focus your investigation on the quality of care provided. If your loved one declines, will this facility be able to adjust to new needs, or would you have to move him elsewhere?
- Downsizing and moving from a long-established home can be overwhelming. Distribute the moving responsibilities among your family caregiving team members so no one is shouldering the entire job. Involve your loved one in discussions about what to take and where to settle belongings in her new home.
- Caregiving won't end with this move, but it will change your role, and you will be making a transition along with your loved one. Be alert for guilt and sadness that may arise for you or other family members as a result of the move. Give your loved one time to get acclimated to his new environment. Do your best not to second-guess the decision, and remember that another move is possible should it prove necessary.

CHAPTER 9

Conscious Caregiving Near the End of Life

Sadly, no matter how wonderful a caregiver you are, even-tually you will have to face the end of your loved one's life. And you will both benefit by talking about it in advance, even though this will likely be difficult. In this chapter, you'll learn how to approach these delicate and heartbreaking topics as well as what hospice means and common misconceptions about it. You will learn how mindful communication can enrich this precious time spent with your loved one and how practicing self-care will help you feel stronger and more resilient. You'll also come to understand anticipatory grief and find guidance on how to navigate through final farewells and funerals.

UNDERSTANDING ANTICIPATORY GRIEF

As a family caregiver, you dedicate countless hours and enormous energy to helping your loved one live at the highest level possible for as long as possible. While doing so, with respect and tender loving care, you will reach the unavoidable end result: at some point your care recipient will die, because all human beings do. Death is a part of life, and this finale is the finish line for caregivers—the ultimate, unsatisfactory outcome. Whether spoken aloud or subconsciously thought about, death is an underlying element that will be part of your caregiving journey. The topic is intense, uncomfortable, and often not addressed by families, even though it's inevitable.

However and whenever death occurs—whether suddenly or expected after a slow, and sometimes painful, decline over time—grieving afterward is a natural and heartfelt reaction to death. But family caregivers may experience feelings of something called anticipatory grief well before a loved one passes, especially if she has an illness like Alzheimer's, a slow, progressive, and so-far-incurable disease.

Anticipatory grief is the feeling of loss that occurs while your loved one is still alive. These painful feelings stem from imagining what life will be like without your loved one and possibly even visualizing her death. And it can begin before you become a hands-on caregiver. For example, it can occur in a mild form when you see that your aging parents are frailer and can't manage the cross-country trips to attend their grandchildren's graduations. Or it can be experienced more intensely if your spouse is diagnosed with a life-threatening disease, and your "golden years" will not be filled with the travel adventures you had planned.

Anticipatory grief can lead caregivers to wish their loved ones would die because they think, *How long can this pain or slow decline possibly continue?* It's normal, understandable, and compassionate to prefer not to witness your loved one's decline or suffering. But these negative thoughts also create feelings of selfishness and guilt in caregivers: *How can I even think that?* or *I must be the cruelest person on earth to want him to die!*

Instead of focusing on your upcoming loss, focus on ways to enrich your interactions with your loved one while you are still able. Some family members use this time to make peace or discuss end-of-life wishes with their care recipients. If you identify feelings you think are anticipatory grief, acknowledge them and do some journal writing, go to a support group meeting, or speak with a clergy member, social worker, or therapist if you haven't done so recently.

Use mindfulness tools to pause, observe, reflect, and then deliberately shift your thoughts toward a more positive mindset. Continue to be vigilant and incorporate self-care activities from your Happiness L.I.S.T. in order to continue this final part of your caregiving journey with increased reserves of inner peace and strength. Take some "me time" to renew your energy. What sounds good to dabble in now? Coloring, knitting, gardening, baking, or stopping by an antique fair? While it may be quicker and easier to carve out time for a comforting, independent activity, try your best not to isolate yourself and shut out people now. Strike a balance between cherished alone time and time spent with friends or family. It will be more difficult to go through the grieving process if you have to first reconnect with people you haven't been in contact with and rebuild your support system after your loved one dies.

"Learn to get in touch with the silence within yourself and know that everything in this life has a purpose, there are no mistakes, no coincidences, all events are blessings given to us to learn from."

—Dr. Elisabeth Kübler-Ross, Swiss-American psychiatrist and author

---

ADDRESSING DIFFICULT END-OF-LIFE ISSUES WITH YOUR LOVED ONE

Talking about death and dying can be unpleasant, and most people would prefer to avoid these conversations completely. It's a reminder of your own mortality, which most people don't want to face. Another thing that makes this process particularly difficult is that, for many family caregivers, this is the first time you are caring for someone approaching the end of her life. Caring for a dying person will bring up a range of intense emotions for everyone on the family caregiving team. These emotions will depend, in part, on the relationships between each family member and your loved one, as well as your family's long interpersonal history.

Even if your care recipient is in relatively good health, her health status can change suddenly overnight. Don't wait until there's a crisis and your loved one can't communicate her wishes to you. And if your loved one is diagnosed with a chronic or life-threatening illness, it's even more important to have these hard discussions sooner versus later. Discussing difficult topics and completing advance care plans early during caregiving with your loved one and family team will result in fewer regrets and greater peace of mind for everyone later. Learning your loved one's desires, beliefs, and values while she can still share them is a priceless gift from your care recipient. It will allow your family caregiving team to navigate more easily through a time of grief with fewer doubts and without second-guessing yourselves.

CONSCIOUS CONNECTIONS

According to a 2013 survey done by The Conversation Project, a nonprofit organization dedicated to helping people talk about their wishes for end-of-life care, 90 percent of people say that talking with their loved ones about end-of-life care is important. But only 27 percent have actually done so.

For example, people near the end of their lives might be admitted to a skilled nursing facility or hospital, which may prove unnecessary, create physical discomfort, and ultimately be of no medical benefit to your loved one. Unless you've already become privy to her wishes to remain at home, your loved one could die in an unfamiliar, institutional environment and experience unnecessary trauma. Listening to your loved one, discussing options, and helping her make end-of-life decisions continues the respect and dignity you've afforded her as a conscious caregiver up to now.

So what should you ask your loved one? It's not easy to do, and your care recipient may not have all the answers right away, but start the discussion about her end-of-life beliefs, goals, and wishes, with topics such as:

End of Life 101

Ask your loved one, "What does a 'good death' mean to you?" Have him describe what that looks like and ask the following questions:

- Where do you want to spend your final months, weeks, or days—at home, in a hospital, in a skilled nursing facility, or in a hospice facility?
- Do you want to use palliative and/or hospice services?
- Do you want to have clergy visits?
- Do you have any special family stories and/or life lessons you want to write or have recorded as a legacy for future generations?

The answers to these questions will lead naturally into the next set of questions to ask your loved one.

Medical Treatments

Gather very specific information about your loved one's treatment wishes. Don't rely only on his advance directive because it doesn't always cover every potential medical decision. For example, my mother's advance directive did not spell out whether she would want a feeding tube if she could no longer swallow. When she was in the late stages of Alzheimer's disease and could no longer talk, I had to make my best guess about what she'd want.

Ask your loved one to answer the following questions:

- Do you want all medical treatments and options continued for as long as possible?
- Are there any treatments you want to refuse or avoid?
- Have you signed a do not resuscitate (DNR), a medical order obtained from your physician stating that you do not want resuscitation attempted if your heart or breathing stops?
- Do you wish to use artificial nutrition and hydration (tube feeding) if you can no longer eat and drink?
- If your lungs aren't functioning properly, do you want a ventilator or respirator used to support or replace this organ?
- How do you want any pain to be managed?

Or if your loved one's state uses the Physician's Orders for Life-Sustaining Treatment (POLST) form, take a look at that instead and make sure that it's completed and signed properly. The POLST usually addresses many of these questions in depth. (See Chapter 6 for more information about the POLST form.)

Documents and Technology

Most people write wills and have estate plans these days. Confirm that your loved one has done so, and learn where these legal documents are kept. In our technology-filled world it's also necessary to be able to access your loved one's online accounts and digital assets, such as websites. Ask your loved one to answer the following questions:

- Do you have a properly executed will, trust, power of attorney for finances, and advance directive for health care in place? Where are these records and documents kept, and how can the designated family member access them (e.g., safe deposit box)?

- Who are your estate attorney, financial planner, and accountant, and where is the contact information for each?
- What computers, tablets, and smartphones do you have, and what are the log-ins and passwords for all?
- If you have social media profiles and other online accounts, what are the log-ins and passwords for each?
- Do you have accounts where online videos and/or photographs are stored, and how can a family member access those?
- Do you want your online and social media presence continued or deleted?

Keep in mind that many major websites and social media networks have policies to take care of a deceased person's accounts. If you don't have your loved one's log-in credentials, it can be a much more difficult process to navigate.

Funeral and Burial Instructions

Ask your loved one if there are any particular funeral or burial instructions she wants carried out. If your loved one can give you as many details as possible about how she envisions the funeral, cremation, or memorial service, it will greatly reduce the pain and stress on your family immediately after she passes away. Ask your loved one to answer the following questions:

- Have you made arrangements for burial or cremation already? If so, where are the pertinent documents detailing your wishes? If not, which option do you prefer?
- What do you want done with your ashes if cremated?
- Do you wish to be buried in a family plot, and where is it located?
- Do you wish to be buried in certain clothing or with any meaningful items?

- Do you prefer a certain funeral home and/or clergy member to conduct the funeral?
- Are there religious rituals you'd like to follow, and how closely?
- Do you have instructions about how you want your funeral designed and conducted?
- If current or former military, do you want those special ceremonies and elements included?
- Whom would you like to be pallbearers?
- Whom would you like to have deliver a eulogy and/or speak at your funeral?
- Is there anyone you don't want attending your funeral?
- Do you want a reception after the funeral service and/or a celebration of life memorial party at a later date?
- Do you have a vision of these receptions you'd like to share?
- Do you want an obituary placed in any particular newspaper(s)?
- Is there anyone in particular you want notified?

Knowing these details will allow you to respect your loved one's wishes and continue caring for him even after death.

Emotions

When nearing the end of life people grapple with many emotions as they detach from the outside world and turn more inward. They may want to work on unresolved matters of the heart in both prior and current relationships, and reflect on the meaning of their existence. To help your loved one process these feelings, ask her to answer the following questions:

- Are there any people you wish to see or speak with now?
- Do you want to make amends with anyone?
- Are there any family disagreements you're worried about?
- Are there any upcoming special family occasions (e.g., a wedding) you hope to attend?

- What are you feeling now? Are you frightened of what death will bring and/or of feeling pain and suffering?
- What can I and other family team members do to ease your anxieties or fears?
- Do you want to be outdoors, read, pray, listen to favorite music, eat favorite foods, or look at cherished family videos or family photo albums?

Don't underestimate the importance of this inner journey. Emotional and spiritual growth can happen right up to the moment a person dies.

CONSCIOUS CONNECTIONS

Why wait until a funeral to express your love for someone and share the positive impact she has had on your life? Have friends and family say or write these wonderful things now to your loved one. And be sure you do it also.

How to Begin the Conversations

When speaking with your loved one about his end-of-life choices, be sure to bring mindfulness into play (see Chapter 4), the same way you would if you were have having any other important conversation. Be aware of all participants' states of being and your immediate surroundings. Speak with your loved one when everyone is feeling well physically and emotionally and your time together is not limited. Talk in a quiet environment where everyone can comfortably share their thoughts aloud, hear well, and focus their attention on what's being expressed.

The timing of and settings for these hard conversations can make an impact on how they turn out. If not rushed by a health crisis, they will take place ideally over several weeks or even months. Don't expect your loved one to have all of the answers ready at once. Allow him time to reflect upon these soul-searching questions.

CONSCIOUS CONNECTIONS

In 2015 the Stanford University School of Medicine initiated the Stanford Letter Project because after many years of research their studies found that people, including doctors, agreed on the importance of having end-of-life conversations but did not know how to initiate the conversations. The What Matters Most Letter is one of three letter templates designed to voice key information and wishes for future care directed to your loved one's doctors, family, and friends. These templates are available for free in multiple languages at http://med.stanford.edu/letter.html.

Remember, your questions originate from a place of care, concern, and respect, so be sure that your body language aligns with your words. Hold hands with your loved one, make eye contact, gently rub his arms or back, or offer a hug as you talk. If you disagree with any of your loved one's choices, be careful not to show judgment outwardly. Remember, it's his life and choices, not yours. If you're the health care proxy, you are expected to act as your loved one's advocate even if you would make different end-of-life choices for yourself. When you sense that your loved one has had enough for that day, close the conversation by expressing your gratitude for his willingness to discuss these important yet difficult questions.

Conversation Starters

A natural conversation starter for this difficult topic would be to bring it up while reminiscing about an ancestor's life. For example, you could say, "Grandpa's buried in XYZ Cemetery, correct? I remember his funeral so clearly because I was only ten years old then, and it was the first one I ever went to. Have you thought about what type of funeral you'd want? Have you made any arrangements anywhere? Can you please share that information with me?"

You could also start the conversation during a time when you're talking about another family member or friend who just died. For example, if your loved one says, "I wouldn't want to die like that," gently ask if she could explain those feelings in more detail.

If you want to be more direct, you could say something like, "We've never spoken about some important 'what ifs' about the end of your life. I'm concerned because I don't know what your wishes are if something happens to you suddenly. Would you mind talking about it with me now?"

In going through this process with your care recipient, you might find yourself pondering your own end-of-life desires and needs. In fact, setting up your own estate planning documents can offer you another way to begin these sensitive conversations with a parent: "Bob and I just set up our wills and family trust with our estate attorney. I was wondering if you've done the same. Could we please talk about that?"

CASE STUDY: Denise and End-of-Life Conversations

One caregiving wife, Denise, explains her practical yet lighthearted approach after her husband, Eric, was diagnosed with Lou Gehrig's disease (ALS) at age fifty-three. She says, "I pulled out a notebook and gave each of us a piece of paper from it. Eric asked, 'What are you doing?' And I said, 'We're going to plan our funerals.' He gave me a snarky look and said, 'You don't need to plan *yours*.' My retort was, 'Seriously? You don't care what kind of flowers *I* like, or what music and readings *I* want? Is it really all about you?!' We laughed, and then Eric said, 'Well, yeah. It *is* all about me.' Then we laughed again and got busy writing down details of what we wanted for our funerals. And you know what? We were *both* surprised by certain things the other one wanted. We really learned more about each other. Then we also had conversations with our two children, ages twenty-one and twenty-three, sharing what we wanted with them. There were tears, lots of tears, but on the day of his funeral, I knew we did what Eric wanted."

Don't be surprised if your initial discussion attempts fail. Let it go and try again another time—perhaps the death of a famous person, family member, or friend will provide an opportunity to try the topic again.

EXERCISE: Review Your Happiness L.I.S.T.

With the awareness that this can be a highly emotionally charged time, it's more important than ever to pick out several actions from your Happiness L.I.S.T. in order to remain calm, stay grounded, and avoid burnout. Your daily routine may be disrupted, so time spent on self-care may need to be shortened, but continue this daily commitment to yourself.

You may not have time to begin a new activity you haven't tried before, so choose an activity that you already enjoy and that appeals to you now. Would a brief walk along a favorite path or doing a jigsaw puzzle with a friend or grandchild shift your mindset to a more tranquil place?

Depending on the time you have available, you may need to modify one of your choices by carrying it out in a different or abbreviated way. For example, instead of meeting a close friend for a meal at a favorite restaurant, ask her to pick up a meal and bring it to you instead. You can create a personal oasis in any setting in this way.

Also keep in mind that having a good cry can be very therapeutic. Do whatever you need to do to shift your mindset to a more positive perspective. It can be done, even with an underlying heavy heart. Don't stop caring for yourself.

HOSPICE AND PALLIATIVE CARE

Hospice is a frightening word to hear because for most people it means the death of a loved one is very near. However, the goal of all hospice programs is to relieve your loved one's symptoms while giving comprehensive comfort care. The philosophy differs from traditional medicine in that attempts to cure your care recipient's illness are stopped and only care that makes your loved one as comfortable as possible is maintained. Hospice aims to make patients feel as alert and comfortable as possible while maintaining their dignity and quality of life. The focus in hospice is not only on a person's physical and medical needs but also includes addressing his or her emotional state and spiritual desires.

Choosing a Hospice Team

An interdisciplinary hospice team will include doctors, nurses, home health aides, social workers, clergy, trained volunteers, and a team manager or coordinator. They are all specially trained in issues surrounding death and dying. Weekly team meetings are held to discuss every patient and modify his or her care plan as needed. Keep in mind, though, that a hospice company is only as good as its staff. Interview two or three different companies to compare their approaches to your loved one's care, and to get a sense about their staff members. You should be able to identify which company's staff you are most comfortable with overall after consulting with them. Follow your instincts, and keep in mind that you are still the main advocate for your loved one. If after enrollment you are dissatisfied with either their approach to patient care or customer service practices, consider changing hospice companies.

CONSCIOUS CONNECTIONS

According to the National Institutes of Health, research shows that families of people who received care through a hospice program were more satisfied with end-of-life care than those who did not have hospice services. Hospice patients are more likely to benefit from pain management and are less likely to undergo unnecessary tests or be given medication they don't need than people who don't use hospice care.

Hospice Doesn't Always Mean Death Is Imminent

Many people believe that putting a loved one on hospice care means her death is imminent, but in reality a hospice candidate doesn't necessarily have to be diagnosed with a life-threatening illness (for example, cancer or Parkinson's disease) to be assessed and enrolled in hospice care. In order to qualify, a patient must receive certifications from two physicians (one of whom is the hospice doctor) that they are terminally ill and have a life expectancy of six months or less. However, some people live for years on hospice care. My father was only on hospice for a few months before his death, while my mother received hospice care for more than two years. Hospice services are reviewed and can be renewed every six months for as long as your care recipient medically needs them. Unfortunately, sometimes people don't start hospice care in time to take advantage of all that it offers.

You Can Do Hospice at Home

You may be surprised to learn that hospice care can be provided in the patient's home, hospital, assisted living community, six-bed residential care facility, or skilled nursing facility. Freestanding hospice centers are an option, but these are not the only places where a patient can receive end-of-life care. Hospice companies can be large, national corporations or smaller, regional businesses. The residential care facility my father was living in had a hospice waiver, so he continued living there while receiving hospice care until he passed away. If your loved one can no longer continue living at home, confirm before move-in day that the eldercare community has a hospice waiver, so you won't have to move your loved one out when he reaches this end-of-life stage. Moving adds another layer of stress that neither you nor your loved one needs during this time.

Your Loved One Can Still Be Hospitalized

Many people think that once their loved one is on hospice, she cannot go to a hospital for any medical treatment. Yes, in general the hospice philosophy is to only provide comfort care to your care recipient and not perform medical treatments to cure his or her illness. However, if the decision is made to take your loved one to the hospital for any reason, you can take her off hospice service before being admitted and then re-enroll in hospice care upon discharge from the hospital.

You Won't Pay Much Out of Pocket

Many think that hospice care is a financial burden for a family. But while hospice care is expensive, patients don't normally pay for it out of pocket. In the US hospice care is covered by Medicare, Medicaid, the Department of Veterans Affairs, most private health insurance companies, and HMOs.

Not every one of your care recipient's medications may be covered, but hospice programs normally cover the cost of all medications related directly to the diagnosis. Hospice staff members will explain financial details clearly to you. If your loved one doesn't have insurance coverage and can't afford hospice, some hospice companies provide care on a sliding scale or free of charge.

Hospice Cares for You Too

While a hospice care team is patient-centered, care services extend to the patient's immediate family, even up to a year after your loved one's death. While your loved one is alive, hospice provides caregiver education and support for the family. After he passes, grief support is offered through chaplain or clergy visits, one-on-one or group counseling sessions, grief workshops and literature, support groups, and more. The hospice staff will follow up throughout the coming year based on your family's needs.

CASE STUDY: Linda and Hospice Care

Along with the additional nursing care my parents received, I was contacted promptly by a social worker and chaplain who offered assistance to my immediate family each time one of my parents enrolled in hospice. After my father died, the hospice social worker kept in touch with me by phone and mail. The hospice company offered bereavement counseling, support groups, and grief workshops. All of these continuing services are free to the family.

I didn't feel I needed grief counseling initially, but as the one-year anniversary of my dad's death approached, I decided to meet with the social worker who'd kept in touch with me. This one-time counseling session gave me some answers to nagging questions weighing on my mind about my dad's final hours and helped me move along in the grieving process.

What Is Palliative Care?

Over the past thirty years, palliative medicine has grown into another end-of-life health care option similar to but different than hospice. Palliative care is for anyone, of any age, who has a long-term, chronic illness, such as cancer, heart failure, diabetes, or kidney disease. It is similar to hospice programs in its multidisciplinary team approach to care, and its focus is on improving the quality of life for a seriously ill patient through the relief of pain and suffering via symptom management. Also like hospice, palliative care addresses the psychological and spiritual needs of care recipients and their families, and it can be provided in any location, including at home, hospitals, skilled nursing facilities, and specialized, outpatient palliative care clinics.

Palliative care differs from hospice care because it can start any time after your care recipient receives a diagnosis, not only when his life expectancy is less than six months, and can continue during the whole illness. Another major difference that separates it from hospice care is that your loved one can receive palliative treatment *and* curative care at the same time.

What proves confusing to people is that many hospice companies offer palliative care programs too. Your loved one's physician, hospital social worker, or hospice company staff member can explain the different care options available to you and your loved one. While Medicare, Medicaid, and most health insurance plans cover all or some palliative care services, there is no broad coverage specific to it, like Medicare hospice benefits.

SAYING GOODBYE

At the end of your loved one's life you and other family members may need to give your loved one "permission" to die, especially if she has suffered for a long time due to a serious or chronic illness. If permission is not given, your loved one may cling to life longer and possibly suffer more. Conscious caregivers use their minds, hearts, and instincts to recognize when the time is right to give their loved ones permission to let go. It will likely go against the grain of *everything* you, as a family caregiver, have strived for, and you may feel uncomfortable or guilty, yet it could be a most compassionate gift. Your loved one may not want to leave you for fear that you won't be taken care of. Tell him that you (and anyone else he is worried about) will be fine and that it's okay to pass on. This reassurance may need to be delivered multiple times by different family members.

Saying goodbye can be important for your care recipient, as well as for you, the family caregiving team, other family members, and friends. Farewells can take many forms—visits, letters, prayers, poetry, phone calls, and online visits via technology. Take your cues from your loved one, if possible, about how to best make these goodbyes happen. Now is the time for everyone to express their love, final thoughts, sadness, and gratitude, in whatever way they choose. Don't wait for a funeral to share all the wonderful things about your loved one—let her know your feelings now.

CASE STUDY: Colleen and Saying Goodbye

During Wayne's last twenty-four hours at home, even though he was unconscious, his daughter, Colleen, placed a big, neon yellow sign right over his head for every visitor to see that read, "Hearing is the last sense to go. Speak as though he can hear you, because he probably can." Why did she do this? She says, "I didn't want anyone saying anything untoward, stupid, or out of line. To me that was *really* important, because there was no way he could respond if he heard something he didn't like."

The hospice nurse with them that night shared important information when Colleen thoughtfully asked her, "What *don't* I know? What am I *not* seeing that will help me?" The nurse told her in little bits what would happen, the signs of dying to watch for, and more. Colleen explains, "For example, there's a medicine that dries up the mucus so you don't hear the death rattle. The nurse said, 'That's for us; it's not for him. It's to make *us* feel better.'" Then a little later, Colleen learned it was the same with the oxygen he was using. "She explained the oxygen was making him breathe more when he didn't want to. The oxygen was for *us*, to make *us* feel better."

During the evening, Colleen slowly changed her dad's course of care, toward what was best for him and not for the people in the room. "I sat next to him and kept a hand on him. Everyone had a hand on him at the end, and he went being loved, period. I'm *so* thankful for that hospice nurse who was generous with her information. You love them so much, you want to do what's best. It comes from love."

Colleen was receptive to the nurse's recommendations to help make Wayne's death as gentle and peaceful as possible *for him*. Hospice nurses, specialists trained in death and dying, are there to guide you and your family during the end of life. Tap into and trust their knowledge and experience.

CHAPTER SUMMARY

The following are takeaways, action steps, and reminders to help you at the end of your caregiving journey.

- During caregiving you could experience anticipatory grief, which is the feeling of loss that occurs while your loved one is still alive. Rather than focusing on the coming loss, enrich your interactions with your loved one now, express your love and gratitude, and use the time to record family stories, ancestry, and recipes.
- As hard as it is to talk about, it's important to learn your loved one's end-of-life preferences, including medical, social, emotional, spiritual, financial, and practical desires, in as much detail as possible. This knowledge will be an immense gift that he gives you and your family, allowing you to know you carried out your loved one's wishes after he is gone.
- Don't be frightened by the word *hospice*. It is a service provided to the patient and her family via a multidisciplinary health care team that focuses on quality of life and compassionate comfort care rather than continuing curative treatment. To qualify, your loved one must receive certifications from two physicians that she is terminally ill and has a life expectancy of six months or less. Hospice companies will provide a free consultation to assess if your loved one qualifies and explain further details of her care.

CHAPTER 10

After Caregiving Ends

When you're caregiving, you're busy. Stressed. Busy. Overwhelmed. Busy. Exhausted. Busy. Heartbroken. Busy, busy, busy! Then your loved one passes, and the intensity of caregiving is gone. How do you grieve? What steps do you take next to make your life meaningful without your loved one? Where do you even begin? The term *new normal* describes in general the results from making adjustments in your life after any drastic change. This chapter teaches you about this new stage of life and gives you the information you need to find the best new normal you can create. Being a conscious caregiver doesn't end with your loved one's death. Here you'll see how mindfulness and self-care practices can help you navigate through the grieving process and rebuild your life.

THE GRIEVING PROCESS

Every person grieves and comes to terms with a loved one's death in his own way and time. Your relationship with your care recipient, your coping style, your culture, your religious beliefs, and the circumstances of your loved one's death will all affect your unique grief and mourning process.

Some people make a distinction between grief and mourning as two separate parts of bereavement. Grief is considered the initial emotional reaction to a loss, and mourning is the expression of grief and learning how to continue on and adapt to this loss in your life. But both grief and mourning are universal experiences shared by people in all cultures. There is no set timetable for how long your grief will last or an exact how-to manual on coping with the emotional pain.

Grieving may feel like a roller coaster ride with no end in sight. One moment you could be crying and, in the next moment, laughing, as you remember a funny time spent with your loved one. You might experience feelings on the spectrum from intense sadness, emptiness, and regret to relief, gratitude, and contentment. There can be physical reactions as well, such as insomnia, a weakened immune system, weight loss or gain, and fatigue.

EXERCISE: Use Mindful Thinking to Cope

Working through a loss is one of the ultimate self-care endeavors of your life. Begin figuring out your unique needs during grief by using mindful thinking to assess how you're feeling *that day*. In fact, right after your loss, focus initially on how you're feeling *that hour*. Pause in whatever you're doing, whether you're home alone or in a group. Repeat what you've mastered as a conscious caregiver and carefully observe your body, thoughts, and feelings by using your five senses.

Depending upon this self-assessment, do whatever you need to do for you at that moment. If you feel discomfort physically, emotionally, or spiritually, change your immediate surroundings (location and/or people) or stop what you're doing until you feel less troubled. You may want to be alone—or not. You may want to cry or talk—to yourself, your deceased loved one, or a close friend or clergy member. You may want to keep your "normal" daily routine or not lift a finger and stay in bed feeling cozy under the blankets.

Repeat this exercise whenever you feel uncomfortable in order to switch to what feels best for you in that moment.

Be extra kind and patient with yourself during mourning. Western society tends to pressure people to "get over" a loss, but resist those messages and take as much time as you need to process your grief. No one knows exactly how you're feeling, nor should they judge your personal healing process and progress. You don't have to "be strong." Give yourself permission to feel your truth, whatever emotions that entails. Just as you shouldn't let anyone else tell you how to grieve, don't compare yourself to others who are in mourning or tell yourself how you should be feeling. For example, don't think, *It's been a month. I should be feeling better by now*, or *Cathy seems to have her life together again. I really need to get mine back on track.*

Keep in mind that stress from your loss and grief could make you physically sick. According to the Mayo Clinic, the most common physical symptoms are trouble eating and sleeping, stomach upsets, and nightmares. Grief can also trigger symptoms that mimic heart problems; this is known as stress-induced cardiomyopathy or broken heart syndrome. Stay acutely tuned in to your body. And should you experience any new or continuous physical ailments, see your doctor immediately.

Five Phases of Grief

Dr. Elisabeth Kübler-Ross, psychiatrist and author of the 1969 groundbreaking book *On Death and Dying*, identified five phases of grief. The book grew from many conversations she had with terminally ill patients about the meaning of death and their emotional reactions to dying. The phases or "stages" of grief that she identified are not necessarily linear, nor will everyone experience all of them. Some stages may overlap or occur together. The five stages she identified are as follows:

Denial

During this stage you struggle with accepting the reality of your loss. Even if you've felt anticipatory grief for many months or even years, you can still experience shock when your loved one's death actually occurs. Right after a loss, it can be hard to even believe it's real. You may cry hysterically, or you could feel numb and not cry at all. If you've lost your spouse, you may become frightened or overwhelmed when thinking about a future alone. You might think you hear or see the person who's just passed. You may be famished or not feel like eating at all.

Especially at first, denial is a way of protecting yourself from emotional pain. One way of coping is to be honest with yourself and others and face the hard fact that your loved one has died. Don't pretend your world is all right when it's not. Express the intense pain and sadness you feel to those who understand and support you.

Anger

During this stage you may find yourself asking, "Why did this happen to me?" or saying things like, "I want him back!" Even if the death is a natural one at an advanced age, you may feel abandoned and resent your loved one for "leaving" you. Then you might feel guilty for being angry with your loved one, and *that* makes you even angrier. Or you look for others to blame for what's happened. You could be angry with yourself or other family members for "not doing enough," the medical team, or God or the universe for taking a loved one away from you. You could find yourself angry at others because they don't mention your loved one's name (likely for fear it will upset you), or you perceive they're moving on with their normal lives and forgetting your loved one too soon.

If you're being "mean," accept the fact that nearly everyone behaves in some abnormal or out-of-character ways when grieving. If you feel like yelling or making a snarky comment to someone, practice mindfulness and express your anger constructively rather than destructively. How? Pause, observe, reflect, and choose to walk away in order to calm down before continuing the interaction. Or try writing a letter or talking aloud to your deceased loved one in order to vent any anger you feel toward him.

Bargaining

This is the "If only . . ." and "What if?" stage, where you try to regain control over an outcome you are helpless to change "What if we'd gotten a second (or third or fourth) opinion?" "If only we didn't move Mom to XYZ facility."

Some caregivers try to strike a deal with God or a higher power to undo the reality of what's happened: "If I volunteer for the rest of my life with the American Cancer Society, can you please bring Dad back and make this not be real?" These are ways you try to negotiate away the pain you're feeling.

If you begin questioning your decisions, repeat this mantra: "I made the best decisions I could with the information I had at that time." Reinforcing this idea through repetition bolsters your self-esteem, helps in acceptance of your loss, and fosters tranquility over turmoil. Try to replace unrealistic bargaining with positive affirmations. For example, "While I wish John were still here with me, I accept that he's not and will find a way to go on."

Depression

You're human, you've loved another person who's passed on, and therefore you hurt. But feeling depressed after the loss of a loved one is different than receiving a diagnosis of clinical depression. The loss of a loved one is a life cycle event like birth or marriage but is accompanied by intense sadness, an appropriate human response. You likely feel the pain of your loss in the depths of your psyche and soul. You may feel empty and too sad to do anything or go anywhere for a while.

It's healthier to get these feelings out than to squash or deny them. Allow yourself to express your grief and despair by crying, yelling, or talking with friends and family, or through journaling or other artistic expressions. Join a grief support group or speak with a clergy member or a therapist to share your thoughts and feelings.

While no one ever completely "gets over" the loss of a loved one, in time your depression will begin to feel less intense and you'll notice you're having longer periods of happier times than sad ones. If this doesn't happen, and acute grief, suffering, and deep despair continue, you may be experiencing complicated grief.

Complicated grief is caused by the loss of a loved one and differs from depression, a continuous feeling of negativity caused by a chemical imbalance in your brain. In complicated grief your natural resilience is compromised, and something is stopping you from coping with your loss. Depression accompanying grief will decrease gradually over time, but complicated grief symptoms will continue for months or years. Signs of complicated grief to look out for can include:

- Inability to perform your normal daily activities
- Neglecting personal hygiene
- Having physical problems recur or new ones arise
- Unwillingness to accept your loved one's death for many months or years after it's occurred
- Abusing alcohol or drugs
- Focusing on little else but your loved one's death
- Withdrawal from friends and social activities
- Losing your sense of purpose in life
- Feeling life isn't worth living without your loved one
- Wishing you had died with your loved one

You may choose to seek help from a doctor, clergy member, therapist, or social worker for the depression accompanying "normal" grief. However, using professional help to resolve complicated grief is a must. It takes a skilled mental health professional using talk therapy and possibly medication to help you process complicated grief and regain your sense of hope and purpose in life.

CONSCIOUS CONNECTIONS

If you have thoughts of suicide, call 911 or the suicide prevention hotline. In the United States, free, confidential help by trained counselors is available 24/7 by calling the National Suicide Prevention Lifeline at 1-800-273-TALK (1-800-273-8255).

Acceptance

In this stage you come to peace with your loss over a period of time. That doesn't mean you like it, but you start restructuring your life without your loved one, thereby creating a new normal. If you've lost your spouse, you may go through a self-discovery process and redefine your identity in some respects. This personal journey can be surprising, and even uplifting, as you face a different future than you had planned. Everyone is changed by the death of a loved one, and it may take time to figure out exactly which ways it has affected you.

Eventually you will feel renewed energy and begin socializing more during this phase. However, just like during other stages of caregiving, you may feel guilty that you are betraying your loved one as you begin to enjoy life again. Know that you are not trying to replace your loved one; you are continuing to live your life, and that can't happen if you're in isolation. Human beings need social contact with other people to thrive, so don't feel guilty as you reestablish connections with prior friends and meet new ones. If you've lost a parent, you may explore new outlets for the time and energy that you previously spent caregiving. This is a prime opportunity to review your Happiness L.I.S.T. for activities to immerse yourself in. You have free time available now to add new ideas to your list and enjoy doing them going forward.

Eventually you will become more and more at peace with your painful loss, but from time to time potential grief "triggers" may pop up. Sadness or feelings of loneliness might come over you years later, even while in the midst of a family celebration, such as a graduation, holiday, or wedding. You may want to anticipate ways to incorporate the memory of your loved one at these events if appropriate.

CONSCIOUS CONNECTIONS

If you lost a parent, you may find comfort by staying in touch with his friends. This may also be beneficial for them, as it's hard on older adults to witness many of their friends dying.

HEALING STEPS

Only you can decide when you're ready to engage in self-care healing actions. Some people begin immediately in small ways while planning their loved one's funeral or memorial. Others need a period of time before they actively pursue these comfort steps. Don't force yourself; just keep checking in via your mindfulness practice to assess if you're ready to proceed. And if you try to take steps and find you're not ready, stop and begin again another time.

First and foremost, take care of your health by trying to get a decent amount of sleep, doing some exercise (even taking a daily, twenty-minute walk may help), taking your medications and/or vitamins, and eating nutritious foods. Because grief can damage your immune system, it's important to keep your energy reserves and nutrition fortified to avoid illness. And you will find it easier to get through each day when your physical health isn't a concern.

Allow other people to pamper you. You learned the benefits and value of allowing others to help while you were a caregiver. Now it's your turn to be a care recipient. Let others shower you with the thoughtfulness and caring you showed your loved one. Accept offers from friends and neighbors for home-cooked meals. Let people run errands for you, make phone calls, and/or do chores you're not ready to tackle. Be open to offers of comfort in all forms while you figure out which are most helpful or pleasurable.

CASE STUDY: Colleen and Healing Help from a Friend

Colleen shares how a friend came to her aid in unexpected ways when her dad died:

"I had a friend who was so smart and connected with what I was going through because she'd experienced great loss herself. After I called to tell her the news, she immediately dropped everything and drove several hours to the house. She bluntly said after her arrival, 'I'll tell you right now, I'm going to be bossy and I'm not going to apologize for it.' She started marshaling people and taking care of all the things that needed to be done before the funeral—made maps, got ice, got food. It was a huge gift I didn't even know I needed because I thought I'd be doing it all. And then, on the morning of the funeral, my friend announced, 'I love you, but I'm going to stay here at the house to take care of things and to receive guests. Here's a pack of Kleenex, here's two Advil—take them now. Here's another two Advil—take them later. And here's two bottles of water because you're going to need it.' It was the perfect thing to do at the perfect time. And now I pay that forward for my friends when they lose their parents."

As Colleen did, acknowledge that this is a difficult time for you, your family, and everyone involved. Some people are uncomfortable at funerals and/or being around those who are grieving and may do or say something unintentionally that you find offensive. Try not to judge anyone harshly during this time, and believe each person is doing the best they can in these circumstances.

Keep in Touch, but Take Time for Yourself As Well

Eventually the people who rally around you will return to their normal routines, and you may find yourself alone again. You may embrace having more "me time" now to work through your loss. Try not to isolate yourself for too long, though, because solitude may also lead to feeling lonely. Keep checking in with yourself mindfully to measure your feelings.

Being with close friends and family with whom you can reminisce about your loved one and your shared history is comforting and healing, even if painful. Some people may hesitate to bring up your loved one's name, so make it clear that you *want* to share your memories and feelings with others who knew and cared about your loved one. On the flip side, don't hesitate to set limits when necessary and let friends know when you want to be alone. Try saying, "I've really enjoyed your company, but I feel the need to lie down now. Let's get together again soon."

Express Your Feelings

Express your feelings, either alone or to others, in various creative ways beyond talking and crying. Create a photo collage. Draw a picture of your loved one in whatever medium you like, or write a poem about her. Listen to music that comforts or uplifts you. For example, every year on the anniversary of her father's death, Colleen writes a "memory story" that reveals a part of who he was and shares it with her family and friends.

Use Your Happiness L.I.S.T.

Once again, refer to your Happiness L.I.S.T. to select a comforting activity. You may need to modify this self-care habit for a period of time if enjoyable activities you previously shared with your loved one don't appeal to you right now. But don't completely stop doing things to soothe your being. Choose what sounds good to you at that moment, and do it for only as long as you're getting a good feeling from it. Think again about taking baby steps. Instead of going into your backyard pottery shack to start a new ceramic project, perhaps read an arts magazine article about ceramics as a way of dipping your feet into this much-loved hobby again. Don't remove any ideas from your L.I.S.T. while grieving, because you may want to partake in them again in the future.

Seek Help

Another healing step is to seek out (or continue) connections with a therapist, your religious community, and/or a grief support group. Remember, it's a sign of strength, not weakness, to ask for and accept help from reliable resources for coping with a loss.

If you're religious, turn to your faith for its insights into death and to gather additional spiritual strength. All religions' burial practices and mourning rituals provide a framework to follow and a community to lean on after a death. If you're questioning your faith because of your loss, connect with a clergy member to discuss your spiritual questions.

CONSCIOUS CONNECTIONS

Don't feel rushed to make major decisions or changes, such as selling a home or leaving your job. You may think you're totally clear-headed, but in looking back on the months following a loss, many caregivers acknowledge that they were really only going through the motions of daily living, were forgetful, or were easily confused. A good guideline is to wait a year if possible before making any major lifestyle changes.

See a therapist skilled in grief counseling or any therapist of your choice to work through your sorrow. If your loved one died in a hospital or skilled nursing facility, the staff can refer you to grief counselors. Remember, as we discussed in Chapter 9, hospice companies provide free bereavement services to family members for up to one year after the death of a loved one.

When you're ready and if it appeals to you, seek out a grief support group. Your doctor or hospital social worker can refer you to one close to home. Some support groups are specialized for a particular group, such as for adults who have lost a spouse, while others focus on the grieving process overall. The same rules that are given in Chapter 2 apply, so refer back to that chapter if you need a refresher on how to evaluate and choose a group you're comfortable with.

FINDING YOUR NEW NORMAL

After caregiving ends is another time of transitions and personal growth. As you heal from your loss, you begin to adjust to the world without your loved one, which then creates a new normal for your life. Every member of your family caregiving team will do this type of rebuilding in different ways, and the person who was the primary caregiver will experience these changes most deeply. Tune in to what your mind and heart need, and follow your desires, or avoid or modify those things you don't feel ready to do yet. Give yourself permission to create a different life in whatever ways you need.

You may decide to return to your career and/or full social calendar you enjoyed before. Some family caregivers benefit from the structure these routines provide. Many companies offer bereavement time off and flexibility when employees are ready to return to work. Ask your human resources department about company policies. And don't feel guilty if you want to start playing bridge with friends or play on your tennis team sooner than what other grieving people may do. They're your decisions to make, so do what feels right for you.

That being said, you may find you need to take baby steps again. For example, you may choose to return to work only part-time or telecommute for a while. Or if you loved going to musicals with your loved one but aren't quite ready to use your season tickets for a play at your favorite theater, try inviting friends over to your home to watch a movie instead. Just dip your toes in the water to see what living feels like again.

You might find that you have a difficult time eating or cooking certain foods, because these favorite dishes evoke strong memories laden with emotion. Although it's been many years since they've passed away, I still can't bring myself to eat one of my parents' favorite desserts. You may even want to shop at different grocery stores for a while if that was an enjoyable activity you shared with your loved one that is too painful to do alone.

Fill Extra Time

You will probably have extra time to fill that you devoted to caregiving previously. To honor your loved one and add a new purpose to life, you may want to volunteer for a charity or organization you and/or your loved one supported.

Which options from your Happiness L.I.S.T. sound good to you right now? Do you want to visit family out of town, take a long-awaited vacation, or "play tourist" in your hometown by visiting a local museum you never got around to seeing? Or do you wish to begin a new hobby or sport you didn't have time for before? Will it bring you pleasure to redecorate certain rooms in your house or simply buy new bedding as a baby step?

Changing Relationships

Part of your new normal can mean changes in your relationships. If you've lost your spouse, you might become the one single person in groups of friends who are all couples, and that will take some adjustment. When invited to events by your friends, even if you don't feel like going, push yourself to accept their invitations for two reasons. First, after you get out of the house and immerse yourself in the event or activity, you will probably find yourself enjoying it. The second reason to accept these invitations is because if you say no too often, you could find that the invitations dwindle or even stop completely. To keep these friends part of your world and continue enjoying these friendships, choose to socialize when asked.

"Don't wish me happiness—I don't expect to be happy all the time; it's gotten beyond that, somehow. Wish me courage and strength and a sense of humor—I will need them all."

—Anne Morrow Lindbergh, American author

The time after caregiving ends can be compared to the "empty nest syndrome" that occurs when children no longer live at home. You've had one clearly defined role for a long time and suddenly it's over. Just like empty nesters manage to do, you will slowly find ways to fill the large void left by your loved one's absence. Be patient and compassionate with yourself and your family team. Take healing actions as each of you creates a new normal. A fulfilling life with family, friends, adventures, and joy awaits you.

CHAPTER SUMMARY

The following are takeaways, action steps, and reminders to help you after your caregiving journey is over.

- Just like caregiving, the grieving process is unique for each individual and family, depending upon your loved one's illness or decline, your relationship with her, the circumstances of her death, your culture, and your religion. Yet grief is a universal emotion people around the world experience. Be extra kind and patient with yourself during this time. Use mindfulness to identify what you need for comfort every day, or even every hour. Don't compare yourself to others mourning the same loss or listen to well-meaning friends who try to tell you what to do or how to feel when it goes against your grain. Caregivers are strong. You will survive this sad time and even thrive again after mourning.
- You can and will rebuild a new normal after caregiving ends. You may need to take baby steps first before you enjoy yourself fully again, but it's important to begin socializing with friends and family. Some people find it helpful to jump back into work and their social life with gusto. Only you can decide what works for you and proceed accordingly.
- Keep pampering yourself your whole life. Choose things to do that nourish your body, mind, and spirit. What activity have you done from your Happiness L.I.S.T. today? Get started now.

CONCLUSION: WHAT LESSONS HAVE YOU LEARNED?

Your family caregiving journey changes you forever. Lessons learned through this multilayered experience remain with you because caregiving is a role you don't simply turn off. It becomes a part of who you are.

Because every caregiving journey is different, each person gleans different insights from it. Take some time to reflect mindfully about your experience and consider what those insights are for you. Think over answers to the following questions, and do not judge yourself in the process. They are not meant to make you feel guilt, anger, or sadness, but rather to help uncover the meaning behind your experiences. You can build on this self-knowledge throughout the rest of your life.

- What have you learned about yourself and others?
- Did you find character traits (strengths and weaknesses) you didn't know you had?
- Did any of your responses to various situations surprise you?
- How did you react in times of stress or during a crisis?
- Did you find you are more or less spiritual and/or religious than before caregiving?

If you'd like to take this a step further, think over these questions with your family team members in mind. What did you learn about each of them? Have your relationships changed based on your shared caregiving experiences, and if so, how?

Also ask yourself and possibly discuss with your team the following:

- What did you learn about your loved one and her life story?
- Do you want to record anything about your loved one or his life for future generations?
- What did you learn through the relationship you forged during the caregiving weeks, months, or years? What did you share with your loved one about yourself and your life that pleases you now?

- How has this experience changed your point of view about different aspects of caregiving?
- What is your perspective on the health care system and professionals?
- Were community eldercare resources available and satisfactory?
- Were assisted living communities, residential care facilities, skilled nursing facilities, adult day services, and/or hospice companies satisfactory, great, or in need of improvement?
- What was your support group experience like?
- What was the best local eldercare support service you utilized overall?
- What is your employer's policies for family caregivers and how can it be improved upon, if at all?

The following questions will help you identify your end-of-life wishes. They're also designed to direct your thinking toward applying what you've learned to help new and current caregivers.

- Has your loved one's death changed your perspective about the end-of-life stage and the grieving process?
- Are you clear on your own wishes? Have you communicated them to family or friends and your primary doctor? Have you decided upon and made all of your final arrangements?
- What was most helpful to you during your mourning period? What will you do for others experiencing grief now that you may not have done before losing your loved one?
- What were the most helpful things other people did or offered you during your caregiving years? How can you pay those forward?
- How can you help others beginning or already on their caregiving journeys?
- What were the most helpful things other people did or offered you during your grief and mourning period? How can you pay those forward?

- Will you explore starting a new career, business, or advocacy or volunteer effort to share the knowledge you've gained?

Whatever your answers are to these questions, I implore you to do two things:

1. Make yourself a priority every day. Live, love, and laugh.
2. Don't overlook any family caregiver you meet who might be sliding unknowingly toward caregiver burnout.

Also continue using the mindfulness techniques and self-care habits learned during your caregiving journey throughout the rest of your life.

AFTERWORD: A TRIBUTE TO FAMILY CAREGIVERS

I wrote this tribute to family caregivers while I was a volunteer support group leader for the Alzheimer's Association in Orange County, California. When you doubt your capabilities as a caregiver, I hope it will raise your spirits and remind you about your many strengths.

What Is Caregiving?

C is for **caring** more for others than for yourself.
A is for **appreciating** that all human beings deserve dignity and respect.
R is for **respite** time you take to refresh your body, mind, and soul.
E is for **excellence** in all you do for your loved ones.
G is for **going the extra mile** day in and day out.
I is for **inventing** creative solutions for challenging situations.
V is for **victory** over negative or self-defeating thoughts.
I is for **inspiring** others to care more deeply about their loved ones.
N is for **not giving up** under extremely trying circumstances.
G is for **gratitude** for the tender loving care you give to others every day.

INDEX

ABOUT THE AUTHOR

Linda Abbit is a family caregiver with more than twenty years of experience and the founder of *Tender Loving Eldercare*, a blog and online community for caregivers. She holds a master's degree in education; worked in the eldercare industry; and continues to be an advocate for older adults, especially those with dementia and Alzheimer's disease. In 2009 she received CareGiving.com's Caregiver of the Year Award. She is a contributing writer at SeniorPlanet.org and also a speaker and consultant about eldercare issues for families and corporations. Join her online community on the *Facebook* page *Tender Loving Eldercare* or follow her on *Twitter* at @LindaAbbit.